Professional *Development* for *Successful* Classrooms

Teaching Reading in the Content Areas

for Elementary Teachers

by Margot Kinberg, Ph.D.

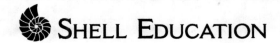

SHELL EDUCATION

Teaching Reading in the Content Areas
for Elementary Teachers

Editor
Maria Elvira Kessler, M.A.

Project Manager
Maria Elvira Kessler, M.A.

Editor-in-Chief
Sharon Coan, M.S. Ed.

Creative Director
Lee Aucoin

Cover Design
Lee Aucoin
Lesley Palmer

Imaging
Phil Garcia

Print Production Manager
Don Tran

Publisher
Corinne Burton, M.A. Ed.

Shell Education

5301 Oceanus Drive
Huntington Beach, CA 92649-1030

www.shelleducation.com

ISBN 978-1-4258-0374-2

©2007 Shell Education
Made in U.S.A
Reprinted 2009

Table of Contents

Table of Contents *(cont.)*

Table of Contents *(cont.)*

Introduction

Many school professionals, even experienced practitioners, see the teaching of reading as the responsibility of the English teacher, the Reading Specialist, or the Resource Room teacher. In elementary schools, teachers usually assume that reading is taught during the reading or Language Arts period, and not at other times. In fact, if you examine the state learning standards for the content area you teach or are planning to teach, you will probably find little mention, if any, of oral and written communication skills except those in the Language Arts standards. Yet, in order for students to do well in any content area, they need to be able to process text, communicate in oral and written form, and associate what they read with the concepts presented in class. All of these skills are literacy skills. So, developing literacy skills also helps students develop their understanding of the content you are teaching.

This book is based on the assumption that learning content requires reading, writing, and oral communication skills. For this reason, there is a strong argument that it is in every teacher's interest to help his/her students develop their literacy skills. That is why this book was written—to help you help your students make the most of what they read, write, hear, and say, particularly in the content area you teach. Integrating literacy skills into your content area does not mean you need to abandon your curriculum or become a reading teacher. Integrating literacy skills across the curriculum can enhance the content you teach in the classroom, while also making students stronger readers.

In this book, you will read about strategies for helping your K–6 students develop their reading, writing, and oral communication skills within the context of the content you teach. These strategies are based on solid research, strong theoretical principles, and the experience of content area teachers. As you learn about these strategies, you will also be developing your ability to match effective strategies with the needs of your particular groups of students.

How This Book Is Organized

Each chapter of this volume addresses a particular literacy skill area, such as, using prior knowledge, questioning, and summarizing. Each chapter begins with a rationale for developing that skill and follows with ways to integrate that skill into your content area. Each chapter concludes with opportunities for you to review and reflect on what you have learned and what it might mean for your own practice.

Chapter 1 describes the overall model of content area reading that we will assume throughout the book. This model will give you an organizer for the chapters that follow. **Chapters 2** through **9** focus on vocabulary development, tapping into prior knowledge, making predictions, self-monitoring, using organizers and visual representations, summarizing, and questioning. **Chapter 10** takes up the topic of writing and the relationship between reading and writing in a balanced approach to teaching literacy in content areas. **Chapter 11** offers ways to integrate these skills into a comprehensive approach to developing literacy in the context of your content area.

Vocabulary Review

In this book, you will be exposed to several terms with which you may or may not already be familiar. Even if you have encountered these words before, you may find that they have different and very specific meanings in the field of education. To organize your thinking before you read this book, note your initial definition of each term. Then, when you have finished reading the book, note your final definition of each term, and see whether your definitions have changed. You will also find the definition of each of these terms in the Glossary.

Term	Initial Definition	Final Definition
active reading		
advance organizer		
Bloom's Taxonomy		
Collaborative Strategic Reading (CSR)		
cooperative learning		
discussion		
expository text		
graphic organizer		
Language Experience		
narrative text		

Term	Initial Definition	Final Definition
prior knowledge		
Question/Answer Relationships (QAR)		
questioning		
Reciprocal Teaching		
scaffold		
schema		
semantic mapping		
situated learning		
summarizing		
think-aloud		

A Three-Phase Model of Reading

One of the most common misconceptions about teaching literacy is that it should be taught separately from the rest of the content you teach. This is one of the reasons many teachers believe that literacy instruction is the English teacher's job. However, let us take a look at some research that offers another perspective on this question. Brown, Collins, and Duguid (1989) and, more recently Lave (1997), argue that concepts we learn cannot be easily decontextualized, or separated from the contexts in which we learn them. These researchers have found that what we learn is a product of the context in which we learn it. As an example, consider your understanding of addition. In real life, you probably do not add numbers out of context, just for the purpose of adding them. You add them for the purpose of balancing a checkbook or estimating the total cost of groceries, for instance. This theory of learning, which is often referred to as ***situated learning***, holds that we learn and know in context. If this is true, then it has important implications for teachers. One implication—the one we'll focus on in this book—is that the teaching of literacy is most effective if it is situated within the context of the content you teach.

In order for the content area teacher to successfully integrate literacy instruction into the curriculum, it is important to understand how reading takes place. This chapter separates the reading process into three phases, as shown in Figure 1.1. We will examine each phase of this model in detail and suggest some strategies for helping students in each phase.

Figure 1.1: A Three-Phase Model of Reading

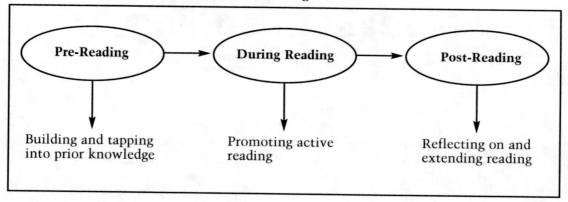

How Does the Three-Phase Model Work?

Phase 1: Pre-Reading

Perhaps the most important concept to keep in mind when students are preparing to read is that, when we read, we associate new information with information we already know, or ***prior knowledge***. Since the time of Piaget, researchers have established that we build *schemas*, or mental representations of what we learn as a way of organizing that prior knowledge. For example, a child's first schema of *dog* might be a furry creature with four legs, a tail, and a bark. As we encounter more information, we adjust our schemas to account for this information. For instance, a child would eventually learn that some dogs are big and some are small, that some dogs have long coats and some short, and that each breed of dog has a different name.

When we read, we tap into our prior knowledge in order to make sense of what we are reading. For example, a student who chooses a book about how to train a dog to participate in a show would access the schema he/she already has about dogs in order to make sense of the information in the book. The student might also access his/her schema of a family pet. This real-world knowledge helps the reader organize the information he/she reads in ways that allow him/her to remember that information.

The challenge for the reader when it comes to prior knowledge is actually twofold. First, the reader may not have prior knowledge about the topic in a text being read. Without this prior knowledge, it is more difficult to make sense of the text. Alternatively, the reader may have prior knowledge, but his/her knowledge may be in a different language if he/she is a learner of English. Second, as the school years go on, the reading material that students encounter undergoes a major shift from *narrative text*, or text that tells a story, to *expository text*, or text that is meant to provide information. Narrative and expository texts differ in the ways in which they are organized and the purposes they serve. Students may have difficulty associating new information they read in an expository text with prior knowledge because they are unfamiliar with the organizing principle of this kind of text. Chapter 6 discusses ways to help students understand and use a variety of text structures and genres; here, the main point is to be aware of the effect that text structure has on students' reading fluency and comprehension.

In order to help students tap into their background knowledge if they have it, or build that knowledge if they don't, effective teachers provide pre-reading activities as a way of introducing students to the topic at hand. You will read in Chapters 3 and 4 about a variety of ways to tap into students' prior knowledge. At this point, it is important merely to understand the importance of doing so.

Phase 2: During Reading

A great deal of research has established that students are not passive vessels into which we pour information. Rather, they actively process what they encounter. Researchers such as Piaget, Vygotsky, Ausubel, and others have shown that learners construct meaning as they encounter new information. They associate what they are learning with what they already know and, where necessary, adjust what they already know.

For the content area teacher, the implication of this understanding of how we learn is that the same construction of meaning that takes place when students, for example, participate in a science lab also takes place when students are reading the text that accompanies the lab. Knowing this, the effective teacher provides students with strategies to develop and check their understanding as they read. You will find that your students have a much easier time remembering what they have read if they have ways of associating that information with what they already know while they are actually reading. In Chapters 5 and 6, you will read about several approaches to guiding students' thinking while they are reading and helping them to monitor their own understanding. You will learn strategies for helping students in both guided reading and independent reading contexts, and you will learn how fiction and nonfiction can be used to help students better understand the concepts they are learning.

Phase 3: Post-Reading

Many people have the mistaken assumption that once a student has finished reading, assuming he/she has understood the material, that he/she is also finished with that material. However, as we will see, students benefit from the opportunity to extend their learning through post-reading activities. These activities are designed to help students apply what they have learned through reading to different contexts. Post-reading activities also help students check their own understanding and can make what they have read meaningful in their own lives.

Making what one reads personally meaningful helps the reader to retain that information longer and in more depth. Why? Research shows that the more associations we have with a concept or piece of information, the more developed and more sophisticated our schemas are of that concept. So, if a learner is reading about a topic with which he/she is personally familiar, he/she is likely to get more meaning from the reading. For instance, Sasaki (2000) found that Japanese students learning English had an easier time understanding an English-language text and responding to questions about it if the text dealt with culturally familiar topics.

What does all of this mean for the content area teacher? Basically, it means that if we give students opportunities to extend their learning after they read, they are more likely to remember what they have read, apply it in their own lives, and use it as they continue to learn. Chapters 8 and 9 show you ways in which you can teach students to check their understanding after they have read and how they can apply that information in new situations.

As we will see, the three-phase model of reading helps students to better comprehend what they read, associate what they read with what they already know, and monitor their own understanding of what they are reading (e.g., Sorrell, 1996). All of this allows students to access the information in their texts and to derive meaning from what they read.

Applying the Three-Phase Model in the Classroom

To better understand how this three-phase model can be implemented in the classroom, let us consider a concrete example. Suppose you are designing a science unit for your second-grade students on categories of animals (mammals, reptiles, fish, birds, and amphibians). Your first lessons will be about mammals, and you will have selected a reading from your students' science book about that topic.

Recall that in the pre-reading phase of a lesson the main goal is to tap into students' prior knowledge. This can be accomplished in a number of ways, depending on the topic and your students. In this case, since the topic is mammals, and students are typically familiar with dogs and cats, you use those animals as examples to tap into students' prior knowledge. Begin by asking your group of students whether anyone has a dog or a cat. Then write the words *dog* and *cat* on a large piece of paper, an overhead transparency, or a whiteboard. Under each word, develop a list of characteristics of dogs and cats with your students. Once that list is finished, have your students note the similarities between cats and dogs (have fur, give birth to live babies, etc.).

From this list, coach students toward the characteristics of mammals and then classify those animals as mammals. Then, add another example of a mammal (people, for instance) to this list to help students avoid misconceptions they might have by thinking that all mammals are like dogs or cats. Now your students have activated their prior knowledge and are ready for the during-reading phase of this lesson.

During reading, students interact with the material and actively process what they read. They also check their understanding as they go along. To encourage this active reading, prepare an activity sheet for your students to use as they read. It would be helpful to include a ***graphic organizer***, or visual depiction of the concept you are teaching, on the activity sheet. A sample graphic organizer appears in Figure 1.2.

Figure 1.2: Sample Graphic Organizer

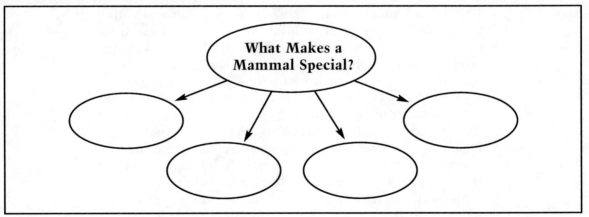

While students read, have them find the information they need to complete the graphic organizer. Using a graphic organizer such as this one helps students to read actively and organize the information they are reading.

When students have finished reading about mammals and have completed their activity sheets, post-reading activities help them check their understanding, extend their learning, and apply what they have learned in new contexts. Post-reading activities can also be very helpful in preparing students for the next topic they will be learning, since one purpose of post-reading activities is to help students connect what they have just read to other knowledge. For example, if your students will be learning about reptiles next, have them use their knowledge about mammals to compare them to reptiles. First, be sure that students have an accurate schema of mammals by going over the activity sheet on mammals as a group. Have students check that they have written the characteristics of mammals mentioned in their reading. While they do this, walk around the room, checking each student's work.

Once this activity is finished, move students to the next step—comparing mammals with reptiles. Get pictures of lizards and snakes from magazines (or by downloading them from the Internet). Choose these pictures carefully to include pictures of reptiles with their eggs. Organize students into small groups and have each group choose a picture. Then, have each group look again at their activity sheets and decide whether the picture they have is of a mammal or of some other type of animal. To close the lesson, note on the whiteboard, overhead projector, or butcher paper each group's decision about its picture and the reasons for their choice. Conclude by congratulating the groups on noticing the differences between the animals in their pictures and mammals. Announce that the animals in the pictures belong to another category that they will be learning more about in class—reptiles.

Conclusion

There are many ways other than the one described above to implement the three phases of reading in your content area. You will read about some of these strategies in later chapters of this book. As you read, consider the following factors as you decide when and how to use a strategy in your class.

One important factor in strategy choice is your student population. Today's classrooms contain a diversity of students, and each student brings different strengths and needs to the reading task. Your knowledge of your students and their needs will help you decide which strategy is the most appropriate.

You will also need to consider the topic you are teaching. Some topics lend themselves easily, for instance, to a graphic organizer such as the one on page 17. Others do not. So, it is important to think about which strategy is the best match to the content and topic you are presenting.

Finally, as you choose strategies for pre-reading, during-reading, and post-reading activities, you will want to consider your resources and materials. What materials do you have that are easily accessible? What technology is available in your classroom? It is important to match the strategies you select with the resources you have or can easily get.

Perhaps the greatest strength of the three-phase model of reading presented here is that it is flexible. This flexibility allows the teacher to adapt the model to meet the needs of his/her students, curriculum, and resources. In the following chapters, you will see how each phase of this model can be implemented in your classroom.

Chapter 1 Reflection

1. What specific literacy skills are most important for understanding the content area you teach?

   _____

   _____

   _____

   _____

2. Make a list of the strategies you use now to prepare your students to read, to guide their reading, and to help them derive meaning from what they have read when they are finished reading. Which ones are successful? Which are not?

   _____

   _____

   _____

   _____

   _____

3. Check the standards or benchmarks your state has established for your content area. Do they include literacy skills? Which ones? If your state standards or benchmarks do not include literacy skills, which literacy skills are emphasized in your state's Language Arts benchmarks or standards?

   _____

   _____

   _____

   _____

PHASE I: PRE-READING

- Building Vocabulary
- Using and Building Prior Knowledge
- Making Predictions and Drawing Inferences

Building Vocabulary

In Chapter 1 you were introduced to the three-phase model of reading. The first of these phases, the pre-reading phase, focuses on accessing students' prior knowledge or building that knowledge if students don't have it already. One very important aspect of prior knowledge is vocabulary. Janet Allen (1999) notes that it is important to realize that when teaching vocabulary, though, words cannot be treated equally, in that each student's prior knowledge makes his/her approach to learning new words different. She further states:

> Research studies have shown that some words can be ignored, some can be figured out in context, some will be known in relation to the reader's background knowledge, and some will be so important that they will need to be learned via conspicuous and explicit strategies. The first step is figuring out what students already know (p. 36).

Furthermore, if students cannot decode new words they read, or if they do not understand the meaning of a word they read, their ability to derive meaning from a text will be hindered. In this chapter, we will take a closer look at why teaching vocabulary is important and offer some strategies for teaching new vocabulary to your students.

Why Teach Vocabulary?

Let's first consider why it is worth the time and effort to teach vocabulary. After all, most textbooks contain glossaries, and many also highlight vocabulary words in other ways. If the information is already there, why take the time to teach it? There are several reasons for teaching vocabulary. One is that students may not know how to use the resources in their textbooks, particulary younger children who are just learning how to use textbooks. Even children who are older or already know how to use their textbook resources may not do so. A textbook's glossary is often in a different place from the passage in which a word first appears. This may mean that a student would have to stop reading when he/she comes to a new word, turn to a different place in the book, read the definition of that word, and then return to the passage. This takes time and, more importantly, interrupts the flow of reading.

Furthermore, using only the glossary to learn vocabulary may restrict the student to a definitional understanding of a word—that is, the word as it exists in a definition. The problem with this is that definitions may not help the reader understand the word as it is used in the context of the passage (Rupley, Logan, & Nichols, 1999). Even if the reader understands the "dictionary meaning" of a word, this may not help him/her use that word to understand the passage being read. This is further complicated by words with multiple meanings.

Another reason for which the teaching of vocabulary is important is its role in comprehension. Children with wider vocabularies find it easier to comprehend more of what they are reading than do children with limited vocabularies. Moreover, students who have strong vocabularies have less difficulty learning unfamiliar words, because those are more likely to be related to words that students already know (Rupley et al., 1999). The importance of vocabulary instruction to comprehension is also the case when students are learning new concepts in the content areas, as Blachowicz, Fisher, and Watts-Taffe (2005) point out: "In the content areas, including Mathematics, Science, and Social Studies, vocabulary instruction is central to the development of new conceptual frameworks and the understanding of increasingly more sophisticated ideas. In short, vocabulary is directly related to knowledge acquisition" (p. 2).

In addition, skills that students use to build their vocabularies also help them with overall comprehension. Harvey and Goudvis (2005), for example, emphasize the importance of teaching students to use context clues to infer the meaning of unfamiliar words and concepts, a skill that is valuable for inferring information about other elements of text, such as titles, headers, and themes. In this way, students are learning skills and not just the definitions of words.

Finally, even if a student is familiar with a vocabulary word, it may have a different meaning in the context being taught. For instance, the adjective *odd* means "unusual" in everyday language. However, in the context of mathematics, *odd* has a very specific meaning—a number that is only divisible by itself and zero. Students benefit greatly when they are explicitly taught meanings for words that are different from the meanings to which they may be accustomed. Nagy (2000) further notes that "[i]f vocabulary instruction is to address this aspect of the complexity of word knowledge, students must not only be taught to choose effectively among the multiple meanings of a word offered in dictionaries, but to expect words to be used with novel shades of meaning" (p. 271).

Strategies for Teaching Vocabulary

Since an understanding of vocabulary is so important to reading comprehension, effective teachers provide explicit instruction in vocabulary. Content area texts include a large number of vocabulary words that are crucial to deriving meaning from the text. Let us now look at three strategies that you can use to introduce your students to vocabulary words they may not know or to broaden their understanding of terms they do know. Keep in mind that these strategies are not your only options. Rather, think of them as some of the many teaching tools that you can use for building background knowledge and increasing students' comprehension.

The Frayer Model

This strategy is focused on a graphic organizer that students use to help them understand the meaning of a concept they are learning and distinguish that concept from others they may know or are learning. The Frayer model (Frayer, Frederick, & Klausmeier, 1969) is especially useful for teaching vocabulary that describes complex concepts or vocabulary that describes concepts students may already know but cannot yet clearly define.

To implement this model, students receive a graphic organizer such as the one in Figure 2.1. Under the teacher's guidance, students first write the word that describes the new concept they are learning, then they write a definition of the concept, characteristics of that concept, examples, and non-examples.

To illustrate how the Frayer model might be used in a classroom, let us look at a concrete example. Suppose you and your fifth-grade students are beginning a unit on statistics. Your goal is for your students to understand the concept of *mean*. Begin class by asking students how many siblings each has and writing their answers on the whiteboard or overhead. Explain that the mean of a group

Figure 2.1: The Frayer Model

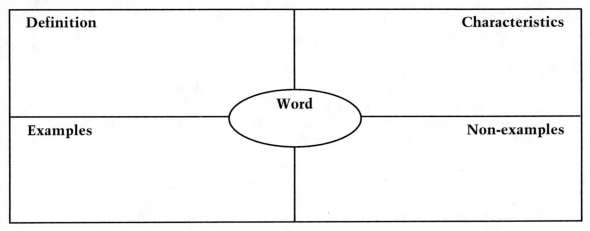

of numbers, such as the ones you have written on the board, provides information about a group of people. Once you have introduced the concept of what a mean is, demonstrate it further by finding the mean number of siblings in your class. Ask your students what they think that number represents. As students brainstorm, coach them to understand that that number represents the *average* number of siblings in the class. You are now ready to use this demonstration to help students work toward their own definitions of the term.

To do this, hand out copies of the Frayer model to your students. Have them write the word *mean* in the center of the diagram. Explain to students that the mean is the sum of a collection of numbers, such as the ones you have written, divided by the amount of numbers in the collection. Once students have a definition, have them write the definition in the top left block on their graphic organizer. Now that they have a definition, students are ready to think about the characteristics of the concept of *mean*. In the top right block of the diagram, students will likely write such characteristics as: average, describes a group of numbers, and so on.

To help students distinguish between the mean and other kinds of aggregate numbers, ask them to give examples of where they see averages, or means. As you get those examples (e.g., a baseball pitcher's Earned Run Average (ERA) or a student's average test score in a class), coach students to place them in the lower left block of their diagrams. Then, have students think of aggregate numbers that are not averages (some examples are the total number of students in a class or the total points each team scores in a game).

Once students have completed their Frayer graphic organizers, have them keep the organizers in their math journals so they can use them again as they compare the concept of *mean* with the concepts of *median* and *mode*.

RIVET

The Frayer model is only one way in which you can help your students develop their vocabulary skills, consequently, you may not wish to use the Frayer model for every vocabulary-building purpose. Sometimes, rather than concept development, your vocabulary goal will be simply to introduce a new word and help students learn to recognize and spell that word. For this purpose, many teachers use a strategy called RIVET (Cunningham, 1999). RIVET is structured like the word game Hangman, and like Hangman, it calls on players to guess words.

Here is how RIVET works: The teacher selects six to eight important vocabulary words from the students' upcoming reading. Then, the teacher draws lines corresponding to each letter in the first word on the whiteboard or overhead projector. On the first line, the teacher writes the first letter of the word, and students try to guess the word. As the teacher adds letters, the students refine their guesses until they figure out what the word is. The process is then repeated for the remaining words. Once all of the words have been guessed correctly, effective teachers use RIVET to help students make predictions about the topic of what they are reading.

To help you get a sense of how RIVET might work in your classroom, consider the following example. You and your third-grade students are working on a social studies unit on geography. Your students are about to read a section in their textbooks that describes a variety of geographic features. You want them to be prepared not only to decode the words for these features, but also to understand the main point of the passage. So, you make a list of the following words: *lake, desert, river, valley, mountain, coastal*. Begin by writing four blank spaces corresponding to the word *lake* on the whiteboard, placing the first letter of the word in the first blank (see the example below), and ask students to guess the word.

L __ __ __

After the first few guesses, add a letter and ask for more guesses.

L A __ __

Once all of the letters have been added, move to the next word and go through the same steps.

L A K E

D E S E R T

R I V E R

V A L L E Y

M O U N T A I N

C O A S T A L

After your students have guessed all the words, ask them to look at the words and predict what the text they are going to read is about.

As you can see, RIVET is a useful strategy for words that students may have heard of and may know, but may not recognize in print. RIVET is also useful as a tool for practicing spelling.

Possible Sentences

Vocabulary building serves a number of purposes when students read. One is that it helps students make predictions about the text they will read. You will read more about making predictions in Chapter 4. For now, let us consider a strategy that helps students build their word knowledge and sharpen their prediction skills at the same time.

Possible Sentences (Moore & Moore, 1992) asks students to combine words they know with new vocabulary words and then to write sentences they think might be in a passage they are about to read. First, the teacher lists a set of words on the whiteboard or overhead, reading each word aloud as it is written. This set includes new vocabulary words and words that students already know. Then, students are asked to create sentences using at least two of the words. As the students share their sentences, the teacher writes them exactly as the students have dictated them. Students then read the passage the teacher has selected, noting carefully which sentences they predicted correctly and which are incorrect. After reading the passage, students go back and correct the sentences that are not accurate.

Possible Sentences allows students to relate new vocabulary words to words they already know. It also allows students to practice making predictions while they build vocabulary. The following example will help you see how Possible Sentences might be implemented in your classroom.

Suppose you and your fourth-grade students are studying the solar system. Your students are about to read the following passage about the planet Mercury:

> *Mercury is the planet closest to the sun. It is a small planet, a little bigger than Earth's moon. Mercury is covered with thousands of dents. The dents are shaped like bowls and are called craters. Craters were made when meteorites crashed into Mercury long ago. A meteorite is a rock from space that has struck the surface of a planet or moon. In 1974, scientists sent the* Mariner 10 *space probe to visit Mercury. A space probe is a vehicle that carries cameras and other tools for studying different objects in space. (Scott, Foresman & Co., 2003, p. 522).*

After reading this passage carefully, select some key words that are important for understanding the passage. Write those words on the whiteboard, reading each one aloud as you write it:

Mercury
planet
moon
surface
dents
craters
meteorite
rock
space probe
vehicle

Next, ask your students to make up sentences using at least two of these words. Here are three sample sentences your students may create (the key words appear in boldface):

> **Mercury** is a **planet**.
>
> A **space probe** visited **Mercury**.
>
> The **moon** has **craters** on it.

Now, have your students carefully read the passage about Mercury, comparing what they read to the sentences they have created. After they are done reading the passage, ask them to look at their sentences again. Which ones need to be revised? Have them revise their sentences; after they have revised their sentences, the students' sentences may look like these:

> **Mercury** is the **planet** closest to the sun.
>
> A **space probe** is a vehicle that carries cameras and other tools for studying different objects in space.
>
> **Craters** were made when **meteorites** crashed into **Mercury** long ago.

Possible Sentences helps students understand new vocabulary words in the context of their reading. This strategy also helps students learn the skill of revising their original predictions and allows them to build vocabulary.

Conclusion

As you have seen, vocabulary building can be integrated into any content area you teach. The vocabulary words you teach and the strategy you use to teach those words will depend on the topic. Some topics lend themselves more easily to some vocabulary strategies than to others. Your content knowledge will help you decide which strategy is the most appropriate.

The decision about which vocabulary words to teach and how to teach them will also depend on the purpose of the vocabulary lesson. Do you want to introduce new words?

New concepts? Do students need to learn prediction skills? As you consider these questions, you will find that you can match the strategy you select to your own needs.

Finally, research clearly shows that once vocabulary is taught, it is crucial to provide repeated exposure to and application of the words (e.g., Beck, McKeown, & Kucan, 2002; National Reading Panel, 2000). Beck, McKeown, and Kucan (2002) stress that the more frequently students encounter new words—in the classroom and beyond—the more likely that these words will become a permanent part of their vocabulary.

Chapter 2 Reflection

1. How will it help your particular students to focus on vocabulary as a pre-reading strategy?

   _____

   _____

   _____

   _____

2. Which vocabulary-building strategy are you most interested in using with your students? Why? What makes that strategy particularly appropriate?

   _____

   _____

   _____

   _____

   _____

3. Using the Internet, find three other vocabulary-building strategies that interest you. What are they and why do they interest you? How can you adapt these strategies for your particular students?

   _____

   _____

   _____

   _____

   _____

Using and Building Prior Knowledge

In Chapter 1, you read about the importance of tapping into students' prior knowledge. In this chapter, we will discuss prior knowledge in more detail, and you will read about strategies you can use in your content area to tap into students' existing schemas. You will also read about ways to build prior knowledge when students do not already have a schema for the material you are teaching.

How Do We Develop Schemas and Prior Knowledge?

Before discussing ways to build and tap into prior knowledge, it is important to consider what prior knowledge is, and why it is such an integral element of the reading process. Since the time of Piaget (1950), studies have demonstrated that humans are active processors of information. That is, we do not simply respond to external stimuli; we actively seek out, sort out, and make meaning from the knowledge that we encounter.

According to Piaget, we acquire knowledge through the development of schemas. We build these schemas in at least three ways. One way is by adding new information to them. Piaget referred to this as *assimilation*, while more recent researchers refer to it as *accretion*. Another way in which we build schemas is by adapting our existing schemas to allow for new information. Piaget used the term *accommodation* to describe this process, while more recent cognitive psychologists refer to it as *tuning*. Finally, we may need to completely change an existing schema if new information is inconsistent with that schema. *Restructuring* is the term most commonly used for that process.

As an example of how schema-building works, let us return to the example presented in Chapter 1 of a child learning about dogs. A child's first schema of *dog* might consist of a furry creature that barks and has four legs and a tail. That schema could have been based on a picture in a book, a dog that a parent or caregiver pointed out during a walk, the family pet, or in some other direct way. As the child encounters other dogs, he/she *assimilates/accretes* his/her schema of *dog* by including different breeds of dogs in that schema. When the child learns about breeds of dogs that do not bark, but make other noises (e.g., the Basenji), he/she *accommodates/tunes* his/her schema of *dog* to allow for this information. Suppose a child's schema of *dog* has been based on an animated movie or television show—he/she might have to *restructure* that schema once he/she learns that real dogs do not talk, walk on their hind legs, or wear clothes.

Why Is Prior Knowledge So Important?

Children come to the classroom with a wealth of schemas for a wide variety of concepts. In other words, they possess a great deal of real-world prior knowledge. As they learn, they add to their prior knowledge and associate what they are learning with that knowledge. The value of prior knowledge, then, is that it provides students with an organizer for new information. The more that prior knowledge is accessed, the better able children are to connect new information to it and recall that information later. In fact, educational psychologist David Ausubel (1968) claimed that prior knowledge is so important that we actually need some sort of ***advance organizer***, or structure, to help us tap into that knowledge before we can really understand new material.

How Can the Content Area Teacher Help Students Tap Into Their Prior Knowledge?

Since prior knowledge is crucial to successfully understanding what we read, it is important for teachers to be familiar with a variety of ways to tap into that knowledge. Content area texts often cover topics students have never formally studied before, therefore it is important to make connections to their prior knowledge from other experiences. There are a number of successful strategies and approaches to help students access their existing schemas. We will take a look at three of those strategies now.

Concept Maps

Concept maps are graphic depictions of concepts and the relationships among them (Ryder & Graves, 2003). These graphics can take many forms, depending on the concept you are teaching, but in general, they show a major concept, together with important subconcepts and the relationships among these subconcepts. To use concept maps effectively, the teacher first identifies the major concept or concepts covered in the students' reading.

Then, the teacher organizes those concepts and arranges them in a graphic display that highlights the hierarchical relationships within the concept. Following this, the teacher presents the concept map to the class and engages the students in adding their own prior knowledge to the concept map. After reading, the concept map is reviewed and refined based on what students have learned.

To illustrate how concept maps can be used in your content area, let's look at an example. You and your fourth-grade students are preparing to read about the three branches of the U.S. government. To prepare your students for this reading, design an organizer such as the one in Figure 3.1.

Figure 3.1: A Concept Map for Understanding the Branches of the Federal Government

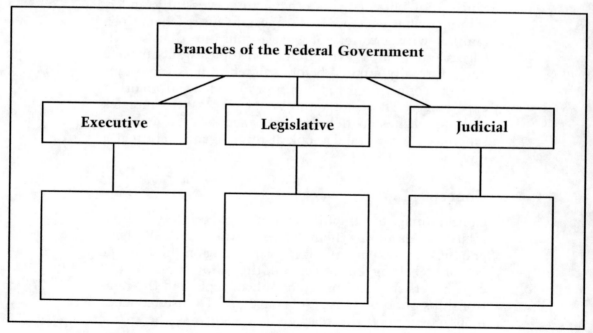

In class, hand out a copy of the organizer to each student. Then, as a class, go over the graphic organizer and ask students to think about what they already know about the government. Then, organize students into small groups and have each group develop its own ideas about what each branch of government does. The groups' ideas are written in the blank boxes below each branch. After this activity, the class reads the section in their textbook that describes the branches of the Federal government and the responsibilities of each branch. After reading this section, the small groups reassemble and students review what they have written in each category and compare it to what they read. Finally, students make revisions to their concept maps.

One advantage of the concept map is that it provides students with the opportunity to access what they already know about the topic you are teaching. Students can also use the concept map as a reminder of the content when they are studying later. Another advantage of the concept map is that it can be easily adapted for any grade level. Finally, the concept map taps into learners' multiple intelligences by providing a visual depiction of the concept you and the students are discussing. We will be discussing visual representations of text in greater detail in Chapter 7. For now, keep in mind that such representations are often very beneficial to students, especially those who are learning English and those who are struggling readers.

Know-Wonder-Learn (KWL) or "What I Know, What I Wonder (or Want to Know), and What I Learned" Charts

KWL charts (Ogle, 1986) are another way to provide students with an organizer to help them associate what they already know about a topic with what they are about to learn. To implement the KWL chart, the teacher begins by identifying a topic or concept. Then, together with the students, he/she creates a chart that divides information about that concept into three categories: what the students already know; what they wonder about (or want to know), and what they have learned after reading. Like concept maps, KWL charts are useful in helping students tap into their prior knowledge before reading and connect that knowledge with what they learn while they are reading.

As an example of how KWL charts can be used in the content areas, consider this scenario. Your second-grade students are about to read an article about fossils and the information they provide to scientists. Before reading, have a short discussion on fossils with your students. During this discussion, write a few of their ideas on the whiteboard. Next, have each student choose a piece of construction paper and write the word *Fossils* at the top of the paper. Then, have your students divide the paper into three sections that are headed with the words *Know*, *Wonder*, and *Learned*, as in Figure 3.2.

Figure 3.2: KWL Chart on Fossils

Know	Wonder	Learned
old You dig for them. Fossils are bones.	Where do fossils come from? How do you know how old they are?	Fossils are the remains of animals and plants. They are made when layers of Earth build up around a dead animal or plant before it has time to decay. Scientists can use the age of the rock where a fossil is found to figure out how old a fossil is.

Have your students work with a partner to fill in the *Know* section of their charts while you walk around the room to answer individual questions. After this, as a whole class, ask students to share some questions they have about fossils and write some of those questions on the whiteboard. Then, ask students to work again with a partner and use the questions on the board to get ideas for filling in the *Wonder* section of their charts. Next, read the article aloud with your students, taking turns reading as you go. When the article is finished, ask students to share some things they have learned while you write their responses on the whiteboard. Give students another opportunity to work with their partners to use those responses to get ideas for filling in the *Learned* section of their KWL charts.

KWL charts have been adapted in several ways for both fiction and nonfiction reading material. These adaptations make them more useful and flexible. For instance, some KWL charts add the category "What I still wonder about" to the basic KWL categories. This allows students to develop follow-up questions that occur to them as a result of reading. Another adaptation is the KWL Plus chart (Carr & Ogle, 1987). In the KWL Plus chart, students review information they have placed in the *Learned* category. They determine which knowledge they are likely to use and categorize that information. These categories of information can then be used to organize students' schemas.

As we have seen, KWL charts are effective approaches to tapping into students' prior knowledge. They can also become sources of prior knowledge for further reading that students do. For instance, if you review Figure 3.2, you will note that students now have a solid base of information about fossils in the *Learned* column of their charts. They can use that information as prior knowledge when they read an article on a topic such as how scientists learn about dinosaurs.

One of the appeals of the KWL chart is its flexibility. This chart can be adapted for a variety of content areas, grade levels, purposes, and genres. Another attraction of this strategy is its value for the English Language Learner (ELL student) and the struggling reader. As researchers such as Krashen (1994) and Cummins (1994) have shown, students who are learning English benefit greatly from opportunities to practice their new language within the context of the content they are learning. They also benefit from *scaffolds*, or learning supports, such as the KWL chart. KWL charts also assist the struggling reader in organizing information and recalling it (e.g., McKenna, 2002).

Anticipation Guides

Another way to help students access their prior knowledge is to have them think about their own opinions on a topic before they read about that topic. One strategy for guiding students in this process is using an Anticipation Guide (Ryder & Graves, 2003). An Anticipation Guide is a set of statements about a topic that students will be learning. Students read each statement and indicate whether they agree or disagree with that statement. Then, students read information about the topic. Following this, they reread the Anticipation Guide to see whether their views have changed. Many teachers who use Anticipation Guides also include class discussions before and after reading, so students can share their views and learn from others' views.

Successful Anticipation Guides include general statements that are likely to provoke agreement or disagreement and that students can respond to without having to read the assigned reading. They also include statements that are supported or refuted by the reading students will do (Duffelmeyer, 1994). In other words, the kind of statements you select for an Anticipation Guide play an important role in its effectiveness, so you will want to frame the statements carefully.

Let us look at an example of how you might use an Anticipation Guide in your content area. Suppose your students are studying bacteria and will be reading a section on the physical characteristics of bacteria in their textbooks. Introduce the topic by having a discussion about bacteria and by providing an Anticipation Guide such as the one in Figure 3.3. After students complete the Anticipation Guide, lead a class discussion that centers on their responses and the reasoning behind those responses. Next, have students read the assigned section of their textbooks in pairs, while you walk around the room answering individual questions and monitoring students' comprehension. When students have finished reading, once again lead a class discussion of the Anticipation Guide, focusing students' attention on ways in which their opinions have or have not changed based on what they read.

Figure 3.3: Sample Anticipation Guide

Read each of the following statements carefully. Check the "Agree" column if you agree with the statement or the "Disagree" column if you disagree with that statement. Then support your opinion in the third column.			
Statements	**Agree**	**Disagree**	**Support for your opinion**
Bacteria consist of two or more cells that multiply over time.			
Some bacteria can make their own food from sunlight.			
All bacteria exist in large clusters.			
Bacteria are not capable of surviving in freezing temperatures.			
Bacteria exist in one of three different shapes; they are either shaped like sticks, balls, or spirals.			

Anticipation Guides are effective ways for students to connect their own opinions and experiences with what they are about to read. Anticipation guides can also be used later to check comprehension of students' reading. Finally, Anticipation Guides are flexible—they can be adapted to a variety of content areas. Although they are more frequently used in middle and upper grades, they can also be adapted for younger students.

When Students Do Not Have Background Knowledge

Tapping into students' background knowledge is, as we have seen, an important part of helping them comprehend what they read. Suppose, though, that students do not have background knowledge about the topic they are about to study. After all, students now come from a variety of cultural, socioeconomic, and linguistic backgrounds. Therefore, it is unlikely that they will all have the same background knowledge and schemas. What can you do to ensure that your students have the prior knowledge they need to comprehend what they read?

The answer to this question depends to a great extent on the sort of background knowledge students need. For example, suppose the knowledge students need is the meaning of vocabulary words they will be reading. You may wish to choose one of the vocabulary-building strategies you read about in Chapter 2 to help them build that knowledge.

What if the prior knowledge that students need is procedural? That is, what if students need to know how to *do* something before they read a text? This is often the case in mathematics textbooks, where procedural knowledge students have (e.g., adding numbers) is necessary for understanding text (e.g., an explanation of how to compute the mean of a set of numbers). In this case, you may wish to demonstrate the procedure students need to know. Under your guidance, students can practice the procedure so that you can ensure that they understand it before they read any text that assumes that knowledge.

Perhaps your students need to know certain facts in order to derive meaning from a text they are going to read. Suppose, for instance, your students are about to read *The Diary of Anne Frank*. You would want them to know some facts about World War II and the Holocaust before they read the book, since it depends on an understanding of that period in history. In cases such as this, many teachers opt for direct instruction. Some teachers make use of handouts with pertinent information; others present the information in a lecture format, a PowerPoint presentation, or a guided discussion. The way in which you choose to present information will depend on the amount of information you are presenting, your students' needs, your resources, and the topic.

Sometimes, when students lack prior knowledge on a topic, the teacher can help them build that knowledge through carefully designed group activities. These shared experiences enable students to use those activities as the basis for further learning on the subject they are exploring.

To illustrate the idea of background-building classroom activities, consider this example. Suppose your students are about to begin a mathematics unit that introduces fractions. You begin the unit with a shared reading of Pat Hutchins' *The Doorbell Rang* (1989). In this story, a mother gives her two children a dozen cookies to share; however, all of their friends begin to stop by. With each visitor, the children need to decide anew how many cookies each child gets until the last visitor, the children's grandmother, arrives bringing more cookies. As you read the book together, stop at the arrival of each new visitor and have your students tell you how many cookies each child will receive. When the story is done, organize your students into small groups and pass out a small plate of cookies to each group. Then, have each group decide how many cookies each child in the group will get and report that number to the class. Now your students would have the background knowledge of dividing a whole into parts that they need to understand what a fraction is and how we express fractions mathematically.

Many teachers build on these shared experiences by having students write about them, and using the students' writing as a class resource. We will discuss writing in more detail in Chapter 10; for now, keep in mind that writing about a class experience helps students build and add to their schemas about the topic at hand. Shared class experiences are particularly beneficial for struggling readers and ELL students—these experiences allow students to connect with the material you are introducing in a variety of ways. Since students are seeing and manipulating the material, they need not rely solely on their reading and writing abilities, which may not be strong yet. Instead, they can use multisensory experiences to support their developing literacy skills.

Conclusion

A great deal of research has shown that we remember new information best, recall it most easily, and can use it most effectively when it is connected with information we already know. So it is in students' best interests when their teacher takes the time to help them tap into their prior knowledge before they read. When students do not have prior knowledge, it is in their interest for the teacher to help them build that knowledge.

There are many ways to help students make the connection between their existing schemas and what they read, or build schemas they need before they read. The decision of which strategies to use will depend on the grade level and content you are teaching, your students' needs, and your goals and objectives.

Chapter 3 Reflection

1. What prior knowledge of schema theory did you have before you read this chapter? In what ways did it help you to derive meaning from what you have just read?

_____

_____

_____

_____

2. Choose a text that your students will be reading soon. What prior knowledge do they need to make sense of that text?

_____

_____

_____

_____

3. Consider the diversity of backgrounds represented in your classroom. In what ways can students from a variety of backgrounds develop the prior knowledge they need to derive meaning from what they read in your class?

_____

_____

_____

_____

Making Predictions and Drawing Inferences

In the last chapter, you read about schema theory and ways in which we organize and add to our knowledge. In this chapter, we will focus on another way in which we use our ability to organize and categorize information—making predictions and inferences. You will find that you can help students prepare for active reading by helping them take advantage of our natural tendency to recognize patterns and make predictions based on them. The first part of the chapter is devoted to a discussion of how we make predictions and inferences, and why this is an integral part of active reading. Then, we will move on to a description of some strategies that you can implement in your classroom to help students develop their skill at making predictions and for testing them later. We will discuss making inferences and ways in which you can help even struggling readers learn the higher-level cognitive skill of inference-making.

How Do We Make Predictions?

Before we discuss classroom strategies, it is important to address the question of how we make predictions in general. You will recall that schema theory predicts that we organize information into related mental representations, and that we add to those representations as we learn new information. Anderson and Pearson (1984) studied the way in which we use our schemas to make predictions; according to these researchers, readers bring abstract knowledge (schemas) to the reading process and use those schemas to draw inferences and make predictions. The process of making predictions and drawing inferences, then, is a natural and important part of successful reading comprehension.

In fact, according to Pressley (2002), one important characteristic of good readers is that they use their ability to predict to skim a text or passage, make hypotheses about the topic of the passage, and draw inferences about the passage. Good readers do this by accessing the prior knowledge they have about the topic at hand and using that knowledge to make predictions about new text. However, not all students are naturally able to recognize patterns and draw inferences when they read.

As Stanovich (1986) points out, poor readers do not read as much or as often as do skilled readers. Therefore, they have less prior knowledge from which to draw when they do read. Reading then continues to be more and more difficult for the struggling reader as time goes on. Moreover, poor readers devote more time to decoding text than they do to using higher-level comprehension skills. Stanovich and others have referred to this phenomenon as "The Matthew Effect," where, in a sense, "the rich get richer and the poor get poorer." According to this perspective, good readers who presumably already have the ability to make and check predictions, tap into their prior knowledge, and learn new vocabulary words tend to read more often. Poor readers, who can most benefit from exposure to a great deal of reading for fluency improvement, often do not get this exposure. Therefore, their skills do not develop, and the gap between good and poor readers increases over time. Teachers are in a position to help close this gap by coaching students in the kinds of higher-level thinking skills that will help them derive more meaning from their reading, such as making predictions and drawing inferences.

Strategies for Helping Students Make Predictions and Draw Inferences

Research clearly supports the value of making predictions and drawing inferences for effective and fluent reading and solid reading comprehension. Moreover, research has shown that poor readers' fluency and comprehension can be greatly improved by instruction in prediction skills (e.g., Edler, 1988). Given the importance of these skills, it benefits students greatly to learn and practice them. In this section of the chapter, we will discuss some strategies that you can use in your content area to promote prediction-making and inference-drawing.

How Do You Know?

"How Do You Know?" is a strategy developed by Richards and Anderson (2003) to model and coach emergent readers on making predictions and drawing inferences. As Richards and Anderson point out, beginning readers often have difficulty drawing inferences from text without coaching. This strategy is designed to provide students with the direct coaching that they need to learn the skills of prediction-making and inference-drawing.

In the first step of How Do You Know?, the teacher carefully selects a high-quality book that lends itself well to drawing inferences. Then, the teacher explains to the class that they are going to learn to understand stories better by learning to make inferences. The teacher defines inferences for students as connections that readers make between parts of a story, or between a story and the pictures that go with the story. Next, the teacher begins to read a story aloud to the class, making sure to stop at a point where an inference can be drawn. At this point, the teacher asks the class a question. When a student answers the question, the teacher asks, "Does the author say that?" When the students respond, "No," the teacher asks, "Then how do you know?" The teacher then has students explain their reasoning, guiding them to make the necessary connections between the relevant portions of the text.

To look more closely at this strategy, consider this scenario. Suppose you and your second-grade students are beginning to read Robert Munsch's (1980) *The Paper Bag Princess.* You explain to your class that they are going to learn how to understand this story really well, because they are going to learn about inferences. Then, you explain that an inference is a link between parts of a story. Once you are sure the students have understood your definition, begin to read the story aloud. After the first page, which introduces Elizabeth, the heroine of the story, you stop and ask, "Did Elizabeth's family have a lot of money?" Your students say, "Yes." You ask, "Does the author say that they're rich?" Your students say, "No." You ask, "Then how do you know?" Your students remind you that Elizabeth "lives in a castle" and "wears expensive princess clothes." You congratulate your students on their good thinking, and continue to read the story, stopping a few more times to ask similar questions that guide students toward making inferences.

Once your students are familiar with the process of making inferences, you can gradually shift the responsibility of looking for inferences to your students (Richards &

Anderson, 2003). Instead of asking questions and then asking, "How do you know?", you can ask students, "What inferences can you draw from this section?" Richards and Anderson also point out that the teacher can provide students with "inference cards" or activity sheets on which students write the inferences they draw and how they made those inferences.

Think-Aloud

Teachers are important role models for students when it comes to reading. After all, the teacher is the "expert reader" in the class. You can use your role as the expert reader to teach students how to use the strategies you use so they too can become expert readers. One way to do this is through the think-aloud strategy (e.g., Oster, 2001). Think-aloud protocols were pioneered by researchers such as Schoenfield (1985), who demonstrated that modeling the process of arriving at a problem's solution was very helpful to students as they learned to select and use appropriate strategies for solving problems in mathematics. Later, this strategy was adapted for use in literacy development.

A think-aloud begins with the teacher mentioning to the students some of the things good readers think about as they read (e.g., facts and what they might mean, predictions, and questions that occur to them as they read). Next, the teacher reads a passage aloud and models his/her thought processes by describing them as the reading goes on. Then, the class has a discussion about the kinds of thought processes the teacher has modeled and how they help the reader understand the story better. Once the students understand the think-aloud process, they are ready to try it themselves under the teacher's guidance. Here, students work in pairs and share their thoughts. Oster (2001) recommends having students write down their thought processes to make management easier. Later, students have a discussion about their thinking and the kinds of things that occurred to them as they read.

You will read more about think-aloud strategies in Chapter 5. For now, here is an example of how you might use think-aloud strategies in your content area. Suppose your sixth-grade students are about to read a section of their mathematics textbook that deals with the order of arithmetic operations. Begin class by introducing the topic of having things in order. Then, explain that this is just as important in mathematics as it is in other subject areas. Then, instruct students to open their textbooks to the section they will be reading. As you read the section on the order of operations aloud, integrate comments on your own thought processes (e.g., "Okay, this says, 'Order of Operations.' I know what it means to put something in order, so this is about putting operations in order. So what do they mean by 'operations'? It says here that addition, subtraction, multiplication and division are the operations, so this must be about the order that you put those in."). After reading the section aloud, stop and discuss with your students the kinds of questions and comments you made. Then, use a think-aloud to guide them through solving a problem that requires proper use of the order of operations. Next, in pairs, have students solve a few more problems using the think-aloud strategy to explain their reasoning. Finally, as a whole class, discuss the students' thought processes. On the whiteboard, write the strategies that helped and did not help as the students went about solving the assigned problems.

The think-aloud strategy has the advantage of providing students with a model for the way experts read and think. Such a model is helpful for all students, but can be especially helpful for struggling readers. Struggling readers may not have learned metacognitive strategies, since they frequently focus much more on decoding words than on getting the overall meaning of a passage (e.g.,

Paris, Wasick, & Turner, 1991). Therefore, modeling for these students and coaching them on metacognitive strategies such as making and testing predictions can help them acquire those skills.

Think-aloud protocols can also be very helpful for ELL students. These students may have higher-level cognitive skills in their own language(s), but they may need coaching in using those skills in English. One way in which you can adapt the think-aloud strategy to be especially helpful for ELL students is to have those students practice the strategy in their own language if they wish. Researchers such as Cummins (1994) have established that using and developing first-language literacy skills is helpful in the development of literacy skills in another language. So, giving ELL students at least some opportunities to use their first language when learning a new language can give them needed support for language development.

Imagine, Elaborate, Predict, Confirm (IEPC)

IEPC was designed by Karen Wood and Clare Endres (2004). This strategy engages students in activities that are designed to help them use their imagination to make connections between their prior knowledge and what they are about to read. IEPC involves the pre-reading, during-reading, and post-reading phases of the reading process, and it involves students actively in the reading they do. This strategy is based on research by Gardner (1999) and other researchers who have established that we think and know in a variety of ways. Because of this diversity, an effective strategy to help students make predictions should involve multimodal and multisensory experiences.

IEPC begins with the teacher selecting the material to be read. This flexible strategy can be used with basals, trade books, other fiction, or content area textbooks. Once the teacher has selected the reading material, he/she explains IEPC to the students by telling them that they are going to use their imaginations to help "create pictures of what they see in their minds" (Wood & Endres, 2004, p. 348). Then, the teacher shares with students that using their imaginations in this way will help them better remember what they read and will help them better connect it to what they already know.

Once students understand the rationale for IEPC, Wood and Endres recommend sharing with students an IEPC form that outlines the four phases of this strategy. On that form, students are asked to: a) Imagine the characters, setting, topic, or events and to think about what they see, taste, hear, or smell; b) Elaborate by giving details about the sensory images they have; c) Predict by using what they imagine will happen in the story or what the reading will be about; d) Confirm that prediction by reading. The teacher passes out a form to each student and displays the form on the overhead or whiteboard as he/she explains each step to the students, answering any questions they may have.

After the students understand the strategy, they can begin to use it. At this point, the teacher introduces the reading to the students. This introduction may take the form of showing the front cover of a book with title and illustration, telling students what a passage will be about, or in some other way letting students know what they will be reading. Then, in the first phases (*Imagine* and *Elaborate*), students can either make notes to themselves or work with a partner to create mental images that occur to them when they think about the reading. After these images have been created and shared, students use them to make a prediction about the story or passage. They then write those predictions in the *Prediction* section of their IEPC forms. Then, students do the reading. This may be done individually, in pairs, or in a whole-group context under the teacher's guidance. Following the reading, the students return to the IEPC form and confirm or revise their original predictions based on what they have learned from the reading.

IEPC can be used at many grade levels and for a variety of types of text. To illustrate more clearly how IEPC works, let us consider a concrete example. Suppose your students are preparing to read *The Diary of Anne Frank*. Begin by introducing IEPC to the class and explaining that this is a strategy that will help them better understand and remember the book, because they are going to use more than one of their senses and their imagination. Pass out IEPC forms such as the one in Figure 4.1 to each student and place your own copy on the overhead, using it as you explain each step to the students.

Figure 4.1: IEPC Form for Use with *The Diary of Anne Frank*

Imagine	Elaborate	Predict	Confirm
What would it be like to live in the Netherlands in the 1940s? Write your ideas and share them with your partner.	Say more about what you see, hear, feel, and taste. Write your ideas and share them with your partner.	What do you think will happen in the first part of the story? Write at least one prediction and share it with your partner.	After reading the first part of the story, think about your prediction. Were you right? What happened in the story that you didn't predict?

Once your students understand how IEPC works, pair them up and ask them to do the *Imagine* and *Elaborate* steps together while you walk around the room to answer questions and ensure that students understand what to do. After students have completed the *Imagine* and *Elaborate* sections of their IEPC forms, stop and have t share some of their ideas as you write them on the whiteboard. Then, have each student make at least one prediction about what will happen at the beginning of the story. This prediction is to be written in the *Prediction* section of the IEPC form. Once the predictions are made, students begin reading the book. After approximately 20 minutes of reading time, stop the class and have students go back and review their prediction(s), making revisions as necessary. End the lesson with a whole-class discussion of students' predictions and what they learned as they read.

IEPC can be adapted for a wide variety of student strengths and needs. For instance, the teacher can adapt this strategy for various reading ability levels. During the *Confirm* phase of IEPC, for example, the teacher may read to the class, or he/she may have students read aloud in pairs, small groups, or individually. IEPC can also be adapted for ELL students—these students might make notes in their own language or read aloud with a reading buddy. They might also illustrate their mental pictures. Struggling readers can also benefit from IEPC. Since the strategy engages students in using more than just reading and writing skills to understand a story or passage, struggling readers can make use of other intelligences to support their reading.

Conclusion

As we have seen, all students, especially struggling readers, benefit from learning how to use their prior knowledge to make predictions and draw inferences. Furthermore, direct instruction in these strategies can help make the difference between a student who is able to read for meaning and one who reads only to "get through it." So, your active, direct, and ongoing coaching in making predictions and drawing inferences can help prepare your students to move from simply repeating facts that they have read to really understanding the material.

Chapter 4 Reflection

1. Do you see a difference between the predicting skills of your strong readers and those of your struggling readers? How do you see this affecting both groups' performances?

   _____

   _____

   _____

   _____

2. Talk to a colleague who teaches at a grade level different from the one you teach. Based on your discussion, how do predicting and inference skills develop over time?

   _____

   _____

   _____

   _____

3. Choose a text, basal, trade book, or other book that you use with your students. In what ways might you introduce this book so that students would be most easily able to draw appropriate inferences and make helpful predictions?

   _____

   _____

   _____

   _____

PHASE II: DURING READING

- Think-Aloud and Self-Monitoring

- Text Structures and Organizers

- Visual Respresentations of Text

Think-Aloud and Self-Monitoring

Up to this point, we have been focusing on helping students prepare to read. These pre-reading activities are, as you have seen, extremely valuable in helping students connect what they already know to what they are about to read. However, recall that pre-reading activities are only one part, albeit an important part, of an effective approach to integrating literacy into the content you teach. In the next few chapters, we will be turning our attention to what students do while they are reading and ways in which you can promote *active reading*, or interacting with a text, in purposeful ways.

In order to help your students become active readers, it is important to understand the assumptions on which active reading is based. One of the major theoretical underpinnings of active reading is *constructivism*, the assumption that learners are not passive receptacles into which knowledge is poured. Rather, the learner seeks to make meaning from what he/she experiences and engages in active manipulation of the information he/she learns (e.g., Applefield, Huber, & Moallem, 2001).

One effective approach to helping your students become more active readers is to coach them to be more aware of their own thinking processes. When students understand their reasoning, they can also be more aware of what they do and do not understand when they read. This awareness helps students and teachers "fill in the gaps," or comprehend more fully what is in a text. In this chapter, we will explore what it means to be aware of one's thinking and monitor one's own comprehension. You will see how this kind of self-awareness can help your students become more proactive as they read. You will also see how being proactive empowers students to take better control of their own learning.

What Self-Monitoring Strategies Do Students Need to Learn?

In order to help your students track their comprehension, it is helpful to be aware of how skilled readers monitor their own reading. In fact, you probably use these strategies yourself, perhaps without really being aware of what you are doing. Let us take a look now at what it means to self monitor.

Skilled readers set a purpose for reading. Setting a purpose allows the reader to develop an overall organizer or mental representation of what the text will be about. Once the reader has this mental representation, he/she can more easily associate information from the text with that representation (see Chapter 3).

Good readers also skim a text first and make predictions about what the text will tell them. You will recall from the last chapter that making predictions allows the reader to tap into his/her prior knowledge. Once students understand how to make and test predictions, they can associate what they read with the predictions they made and thus with their prior knowledge.

Besides setting a purpose for reading and making predictions, good readers ask questions as they read. We will discuss questioning in detail in Chapter 9. For the purposes of this chapter, our focus is on questions that students ask themselves as they read. Answering one's own questions is a powerful tool for monitoring one's own understanding.

During reading, skilled readers also think aloud. As you read in Chapter 3, think-aloud strategies enable the reader to trace his/her thinking processes. When those processes are not successful, think-aloud strategies point this out quickly, so the reader can make repairs.

Another tool that skilled readers use is *paraphrasing* what they read. Paraphrasing allows the reader to check whether he/she has thoroughly understood the author's message. The more accurate and detailed the paraphrase, the more likely it is that the reader has understood the text.

Sometimes even highly skilled readers encounter a word, sentence, phrase, or passage they don't understand. When this happens, good readers make use of repair strategies. These strategies help them to be aware of when they haven't understood what they read, so that they can go back and fill in the gaps.

Teaching Self-Monitoring Strategies

Direct Instruction

Studies of reading comprehension have shown that direct instruction of self-monitoring strategies helps students to better recall what they have read and make more meaning from it (e.g., Preul & Dewitz, 1986). So, it is a valuable investment of your class time to directly model and coach self-monitoring strategies.

One of the most important things to remember as you introduce self-monitoring strategies is that your students will look to you as a role model. Your explanation and demonstration of the self-monitoring skills you are teaching will give students a clear mental representation of how the skilled reader actively ensures that he/she understands the text.

As a way of looking at direct instruction of self-monitoring strategies, let us consider the skill of understanding the main idea of a passage. When the reader understands the main idea of a passage, he/she can better associate that idea with his/her prior knowledge. Researchers such as Baumann (1984) have shown that one effective approach to direct instruction in understanding the main idea is to begin with a demonstration. Here, the teacher tells the students they will be learning how to identify the main idea of a passage. Then, he/she presents the steps of looking for the main idea (e.g., looking at the topic sentences and looking for headings and subheadings). It is often helpful to provide these steps on a handout or leave them posted on a classroom wall so that students can refer to them as needed. Next, the teacher models and demonstrates the strategy so that students can see how it is done. One way to do this is to have a passage prepared on a transparency and to use a think-aloud strategy to go through the steps of finding its main idea. Once students are clear about the steps involved in finding the main idea and have seen the teacher's model, the teacher guides them in practicing the strategy themselves. For instance, you may provide students with a passage on a handout or have individual students come to the whiteboard and go through the steps as you coach. After most students have shown that they understand the steps, the teacher moves on, allowing students to practice the strategy themselves. Some teachers pair students up, while others have students work individually or in small groups. Your decision about how to gradually move students toward working independently will depend on your students' grade, age, ability levels, the text you are using, and your goals, among other things. The main goal here is that students practice finding the main idea of a passage without your direct guidance, but with your assistance if needed. When students have shown that they can find the main idea of a passage, you can integrate this task into your regular during-reading activities, so that students can maintain that skill.

Purpose-Setting Discussions

As you have seen, skilled readers set a purpose for their reading. That purpose guides the reader to look for relevant information and accomplish his/her reading goal. Unfortunately, many students read because "the teacher made them" or because "it's for homework." It is far more helpful to students if they learn to set their own purposes for reading, and if those purposes have more to do with the information they will learn than with a teacher-initiated requirement.

One way to guide students towards setting a purpose for their reading is the Purpose-Setting Discussion (Ryder & Graves, 2003). This is a discussion that centers around the theme students will be reading about; it helps students develop questions they will answer as they read. Those answers then become the purpose for reading. To see how Purpose-Setting Discussions work, let us consider this scenario. Suppose your second-grade students are about to read a section of their textbooks that describes how governments work and who makes laws at the city, state, and national levels. To help your students set a purpose for this reading, begin with these questions: "Why do people stop at traffic lights? Why do they pay their taxes? Why do we buy groceries instead of just taking them?" Once you have guided students to understand that we have laws that govern those actions, ask this question, "Where do those laws come from?" Then, after your students respond to your question, explain to them that they are about to read about where our laws come from and who is "in charge." Now your students have a purpose for their reading—this purpose helps them to read actively and interact with the text to answer their questions. Pair students up and have them read aloud to each other, taking turns as they go. When students are finished reading the passage, have the pairs offer their answers as to where laws come from and who makes them.

When Comprehension Breaks Down: Teaching Repair Strategies

One advantage of self-monitoring is that the reader knows when he/she has not understood something in a text. This awareness allows the reader to go back over the material so as to comprehend it better. Skilled readers are familiar with and use several strategies to repair their comprehension. Some of these are rereading, looking up unknown words, seeking assistance, and reading ahead (Texas Education Agency, 2002). The decision about which strategy to use depends on the specific problem the reader is having. Capable readers use self-monitoring to decide which problem they are having with comprehension and which strategy is most likely to be useful.

Let us now look at some ways in which you can teach your students to be aware of whether they understand what they are reading and how to support themselves if they do not understand.

Direct Instruction

As you read earlier in this chapter, students can often benefit greatly from explicit coaching in how to use metacognitive strategies. This is especially true if they are learning to use a strategy for the first time. When you demonstrate a strategy, guide students in using it, allow them to practice it independently, and then review the strategy, you provide students with a solid knowledge base about that strategy.

Direct instruction tends to be an efficient and effective way to present metacognition skills, especially for struggling readers (Kameenui, 1993). These students often focus more on decoding than they do on comprehension, so they may very well not be aware of what they do and do not understand within a passage.

Direct instruction also has the advantage of being flexible. You can easily adapt direct instruction for any strategy that you are teaching. You can also adapt direct instruction to meet the needs of students at nearly any grade or ability level.

Think-Aloud

While direct instruction can be useful in teaching self-monitoring strategies, one of its disadvantages is that it does not allow students to clearly see the thought processes that expert readers use to monitor their comprehension. In Chapter 3, you read about the importance of the teacher as the expert reader. Your model of comprehension and repair strategies is just as valuable to students as is your model of making predictions and drawing inferences. With this in mind, many teachers use a think-aloud protocol when they are teaching students what to do when they don't understand a text.

Let us look at an example of how you might use thinking aloud to demonstrate the repair strategy of rereading a difficult passage. Suppose you and your third-grade students are studying dinosaurs and fossils. Because you know that some of your students will have difficulty decoding such words as *paleontologist*, *velociraptor*, and *carboniferous*, you engage them in some pre-reading vocabulary activities (see Chapter 2) so they will be familiar with the terms. Begin to read aloud the section of their science textbook that discusses ways in which paleontologists use fossils to reconstruct dinosaurs and hypothesize about them. As you read, you come to the word *paleontologists*. As you read the word, stop and say, "Paleontologists . . . hmm . . . I know I've heard that word, but I forget what it means. Let me just read this sentence again; maybe it will remind me . . . . There it is, 'Fossils are excavated (dug up) by paleontologists, scientists who study ancient forms of life.'"

After you have provided this model, read on for one more paragraph and then stop to be certain that your students have understood the passage you have read. Then, pair your students up to continue reading aloud to each other. As they do so, walk around the room, encouraging them to reread when you see that they have difficulty comprehending a word or phrase. Once your students have seen your model of rereading and have practiced it themselves, they can add that strategy to their own repertoire and use it in small-group, paired, or individual reading.

Scaffolds

As you read in Chapter 3, scaffolds provide students with support for their learning. These supports are designed to be temporary, and they serve the purpose of assisting the student until he/she can complete a task independently. Scaffolds can take many forms; some of these are handouts, wall charts, graphic organizers, and verbal reminders. Your choice of which scaffold to provide for your students depends upon the skill(s) they need to learn and the context (at home, in the classroom, etc.) in which they are developing their skills.

You can use scaffolds to remind your students of what to do when they don't understand what they are reading.

Here is a specific example of how a scaffold might help students as they learn to repair a breakdown in math comprehension. Your fifth-grade students are learning about graphing points and ordered pairs on a coordinate plane. After introducing the topic and helping students access their prior knowledge (see Chapter 2), hand out a "reminder sheet" such as the one in Figure 5.1 to each student.

Figure 5.1: Sample Reminder Sheet

My "I don't get it" Bag of Tricks

1. Go back and read the sentence or paragraph again, really carefully.

2. Read the next section to see if there is an explanation there.

3. Look up words you don't know in the glossary or the dictionary.

4. Look at the example problem to see if you understand after reading it.

5. Ask a reading buddy for help.

6. If you still don't understand after you have tried all of these strategies, ask me for help.

Have your students tape the reminder sheet into their math journals, so they will have it handy when they read and do problems independently. Then, have students silently read the first passage in their texts that discusses coordinate planes. As they read, walk around the room, reminding students as necessary to use the strategies you have suggested. When students are finished reading, have them work in small groups to summarize what they just read (We will discuss summarization in more detail in Chapter 8.). Use these summaries to ensure that students have understood the text. Then, assign a new section of text, with a few companion problems for students to work on independently for homework. As you give this assignment, remind students to refer to their "bag of tricks" if they have trouble understanding what they read. The reminder sheet could be taped into students' folders for any other content areas in which they need this kind of self support.

Conclusion

Research shows that when we have a "feeling of knowing," or a sense that we are familiar with a topic, we are likely to spend more time associating the topic we are reading about with what we already know. Our awareness of how familiar we are with a topic also seems to regulate whether we are likely to answer a question about a topic and the sort of answer we are likely to give (Miner & Reder, 1996). So, when students are taught to be aware of their thought processes, they also become more aware of how they associate what they are reading with what they know, and they spend more time answering questions they may have, connecting new information with prior knowledge.

Learning to monitor comprehension also allows your students to read more independently and to be aware of what they do and do not understand. This helps students to read more efficiently and be more proactive when they have questions or have trouble comprehending what they are reading. So it is to your advantage, and to that of your students, to invest class time in coaching them in metacognitive strategies.

Chapter 5 Reflection

1. As you were reading this chapter, what metacogntive strategies did you use? In what ways did they help you?

   _____

   _____

   _____

   _____

2. With which self-monitoring strategies do your students have the most difficulty? How does this affect their comprehension?

   _____

   _____

   _____

   _____

   _____

3. What other effects have you noticed on your students' ability to monitor their thinking? For instance, is their monitoring affected by ability level? By topic? By type of text?

   _____

   _____

   _____

   _____

   _____

Text Structures and Organizers

Constructivist assumptions are consistent with research by Piaget and other cognitive psychologists who, as you will recall, have shown that we organize information that we learn into mental representations (see Chapter 3). This seems to be as true of information we encounter through reading as it is of any other information we learn. So it benefits the reader, especially the inexperienced reader, to have a sense of a text's structure as he/she reads. Why? Because knowing the way in which a text is structured helps the reader organize the information in the text and associate that material more quickly with his/her prior knowledge.

In this chapter, you will read about some strategies for helping your students learn about a variety of text structures and make the most of each kind of structure they encounter. We will also present some ways to help students make use of textbook resources such as maps, charts, graphs, and glossaries.

What Sorts of Text Structures Do Students Need to Learn to Use?

Your students will encounter a variety of text structures as they move on in their school years. These structures fall under two very general categories: narrative and expository text. Let us take a look at narrative text first. You will recall from Chapter 1 that the purpose of narrative text is to tell a story. Narrative texts can take a variety of forms, from personal anecdotes to full-length novels. However, most narrative texts have in common certain elements such as characters, setting, and plot. Structurally, most narrative texts have a beginning, where the characters and setting are introduced; a middle, where the plot unfolds; and an end, where any conflicts are resolved (or at least addressed).

As students move on in their school years, the reading they do makes an important shift from narrative text to expository text. As you read in Chapter 1, the purpose of expository text is to relay information. The most familiar kind of expository text for most people is the textbook, but there are many other ways in which expository text is presented. Some examples are newspaper articles, responsible Internet websites, instruction sheets, and reports. Unlike most narrative texts, expository texts can have a variety of structures. For instance, such a text can have a question/answer structure, a cause/effect structure, a problem/solution structure, or a chronological structure. Duke and Bennett-Armistead (2003) point out that exposing students in primary classrooms to different information text structures is key to their academic success, especially since it is the kind of reading they will rely more and more on as they proceed through the years.

As students make the move from reading mostly narrative text to reading mostly expository text, they also need to learn how to use the structure of the expository text to get information. They also need to learn to be sensitive to cues in the text that will let them know what kind of structure that text has. This sensitivity to text isn't inherent, so it's in your students' interest to be directly coached on how to be aware of text structure and how to use that information to make meaning from a reading. In addition to teaching students *how* to use expository text, teachers should provide a *why* by creating authentic purposes for reading expository text, such as having students find information about the life cycles of frogs before setting up a classroom tadpole tank (Duke, 2004). Let us examine some strategies that you can use to teach your students to make the most of the structure of their texts.

Strategies for Working With Narrative Text Structure

Many students bring some prior knowledge about narrative text to the classroom. This may be because their parents or caregivers have read to them, their culture has an oral tradition of storytelling, or they have encountered stories on television shows or in movies. The key is to help your students recognize and identify the story elements with which they are already likely familiar.

Story Retelling

Children's ability to narrate a story is an indicator of later skill at language and literacy (De Temple & Tabors, 1996). So, helping your students develop their retelling skills is a valuable investment of time, especially for those students who do not come from a print-rich environment. Story retelling also provides the teacher with a very useful assessment tool; you can use your students' narration to find out which parts of a story they found easy and which parts were more difficult for them.

One strong advantage of story retelling is that it's easy to implement in your classroom. After the teacher reads aloud a story, article, or passage from a textbook, students are asked to retell what they have just learned. Students can retell in individual conferencing sessions with the teacher, in small groups, in pairs, or as part of a whole-class activity. Your decision of how to implement retelling will depend upon the number of students you have, the content you are teaching, and the grade level you teach, among other things.

As you can see, another advantage of retelling is that it is flexible. Story retelling can be implemented at a variety of grade levels and can be conducted in oral or written form, in a whole class, small group/pair, or individualized context. Story retelling also has the appeal of being a valuable scaffold for struggling readers and ELL students. These students can benefit greatly from the models their peers provide. They can also benefit from the experience of organizing their own thoughts without the challenge of decoding text at the same time.

Story Mapping

Story mapping (e.g., Beck & McKeown, 1981) allows students to visually organize the characters and events in a narrative text. As we will see in Chapter 7, visual representations of text provide very helpful scaffolds for students and allow them to tap into their multiple intelligences as they make meaning. Story mapping can take a variety of forms, depending upon the age/grade level of the students, the narrative element(s) they are studying, and the purpose of the reading.

In general, story mapping is implemented in this way: the teacher gives each student a diagram to help students organize their reading. That diagram focuses on elements such as characters, plot, and setting for older students, and the beginning, middle, and end of a story for beginning readers. Next, the teacher explains the use of the story map, perhaps modeling how to complete a part of the diagram. Then, students read the text independently or in pairs. As they read, they complete the story map. The map can later be used for assessment, for studying, or as a source of prior knowledge for further work.

Here is an example of how story mapping might be implemented in your classroom. Suppose your fourth-grade students are about to read *Charlotte's Web*. You and your class have already done some pre-reading activities to give them some background information on the book. Begin class by introducing the book and having students give you some ideas about the setting and offer some predictions about the plot. Then, hand a story map for Chapter 1 such as the one in Figure 6.1 to each student. Place your own copy of the story map on the overhead projector and briefly explain to students how to use

Figure 6.1 Sample Story Map for *Charlotte's Web*

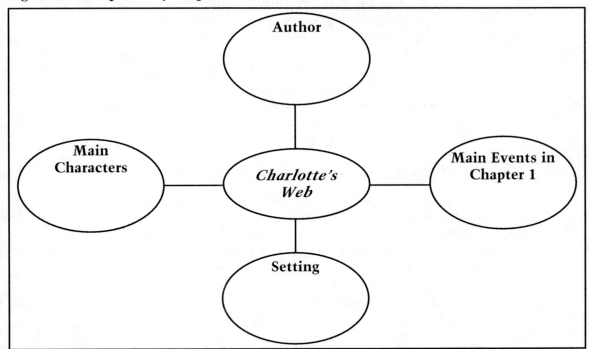

it. Then have students begin to read individually. As they read, have them fill in their charts. Approximately ten minutes before the end of class, ask the students to help you fill in the story map. Go over each element in the story map, asking different students for the information. Now, students have a guide to help them review the chapter and background information to use as they move on to the next chapter.

Story maps are flexible enough to be used as during-reading guides for both narrative and expository texts, and can be adapted for a variety of grade levels and reading ability levels.

Strategies for Working With Expository Text Structure

So far in this chapter, we have looked at some strategies for helping students make meaning from the structure of narrative texts. However, as was mentioned at the beginning of the chapter, many students have difficulty when they make the move from reading narrative to reading expository text. It is therefore often beneficial to them to have your direct coaching as they learn to recognize and use a variety of different structures. Let us now examine some useful strategies for helping your students learn to read a variety of expository texts.

Signal Words

Text structures can often be identified by signal words, which are key words that inform the reader of what sort of structure a text has. Once students know what the various text structures are and which signal words are associated with each structure, they can use those words as clues to the structure. Figure 6.2 shows some of the most common text structures with some key words associated with each (Richgels, Mcgee, & Slaton, 1989).

Figure 6.2: Common Text Structures and Signal Words

Description	Collection	Causation and Problem/Solution	Comparison/ Contrast
This text structure combines similar ideas. A common example might be an extended and detailed definition of a concept.	This text structure groups concepts in a logical way, usually in order. A common example might be a description of the way in which cells undergo meiosis.	These two text structures link concepts or events causally. In both text structures, one event or idea leads to the next. A common example might be an explanation of the reasons for the signing of the U.S. Declaration of Independence.	As the name implies, this text structure defines concepts by relating them to other like or unlike concepts. A common example might be a discussion of the similarities between percents and ratios, or the difference between circles and other geometric forms.
	Some Signal Words: *first, following, later, next, then, ultimately*	**Some Signal Words:** *as a result of, because, due to, since, so that, solution, solve, therefore*	**Some Signal Words:** *akin to, alike, compare(d), different, like, same, unlike*

When students have a sense of the text structure they are reading, they can make predictions about the text and better associate the ideas they are reading. This, in turn, can lead to better recall later.

Since students may not be familiar with these text structures at first, it is in their best interest if the teacher begins by providing some direct instruction (Ryder & Graves, 2003). First, the teacher distributes a list of the different text structures students are likely to encounter, together with some examples of each structure and a set of the signal words associated with each (see Figure 6.2). Then, the teacher explains the value of knowing signal words and text structures in remembering what one reads. Following this, the teacher gives pairs or small groups of students a short passage in which signal words have been underlined or highlighted. Students use those words to identify the text structure of the passage. Then, each group or pair reports its findings to the class. The teacher can follow these activities by having students read various passages in their texts and identify the text structure of each passage. Finally, the teacher leads a discussion on ways in which recognizing a variety of text structures can help students make meaning more easily from their reading.

Here is an example of how you might implement a lesson in signal words in your class. Suppose your students are about to read a chapter in their mathematics text on how to find the circumference of a circle. After a brief explanation of text structures and signal words, give each student a copy of a short passage from the chapter they are about to read. This passage explains that, since circles do not have sides in the way that squares and rectangles do, measuring them is done in a different way. In small groups, your students note the signal words in the passage that indicate that this is a comparison/contrast structure. When the groups have established what kind of text structure is represented by the passage, have each group explain its choice. Next, have a brief discussion of the kind of information one can get by comparing/contrasting text structures. Then have students silently read the passage again, this time for the purpose of understanding its meaning. End the lesson with a brief discussion of the main points of the passage.

Text Structure Questions

Once students are familiar with the different text structures they are likely to encounter, the teacher can coach them in developing questions that are addressed in each type of text structure (Ryder & Graves, 2003). These questions can prompt active and engaged reading, as students search for the answers to the questions while they read.

As we will see in Chapter 9, generating and answering questions is a highly effective approach to helping your students process what they read in an engaged and active way. Using text structure questions is one way to implement questioning in your content area.

To integrate text structure questions, the teacher begins by providing students with a set of questions that are suggested by the text structures they encounter. These questions focus on the signal words associated with each text structure. Once they have the questions, students read a passage, answering the questions as they read. Later, the teacher leads a discussion about the text structure that is associated with each question. That discussion centers on the kinds of information that students can glean from the various text structures, and ways in which to use text structure to guide their thinking.

Let us consider an example of how you might integrate text structure questions into your content teaching. Your sixth-grade social studies class is beginning a unit on Ancient Mesopotamia. You have pre-read the first chapter of the unit and have determined that the two text structures that are most prevalent are description (specifically, where Ancient Mesopotamia was located and when that civilization flourished) and cause/effect (specifically, why humans gathered in cities in Ancient Mesopotamia). After you have introduced the unit, and before students have read the chapter, hand out some text structure questions such as those in Figure 6.3. Write these questions on a large piece of chart paper that you have taped onto your whiteboard.

After you have handed out the questions, go over them briefly, using the larger copy as a model. Then, in pairs, have students read the first few sections of the chapter, stopping to answer the questions as they go along. When students have finished reading the sections you have assigned, review their responses as a class. As you go over the students' answers, have individual students

Figure 6.3: Sample Text Structure Questions for a Unit on Ancient Mesopotamia

Text Structure	Questions	Your Answer
Description	When did this civilization develop? Where did these cities flourish?	
Cause/Effect	Why did this civilization develop there? What were some results of people gathering in cities?	

write their responses on the chart paper in front of the class. End the lesson with a brief discussion of the kinds of information students learned. For this activity, write the words *Description* and *Cause/Effect* on the whiteboard and list the types of information that each text structure provides as students mention them.

Using Textbook Resources

How can students benefit from direct instruction in using textbook resources? As students add expository text reading to their repertoire of literacy skills, they need to learn more than just new text structures. They also need to learn how to use the variety of resources available in today's textbooks. For instance, many textbooks provide tables of contents, glossaries, indices, illustrations such as maps and graphs, links to Internet resources, and within-text cues such as headings and subheadings or bold/italicized words. The better equipped your students are to take advantage of these resources, the better prepared they will be to gather information and associate it with what they already know.

There is another important reason for which you will want your students to be comfortable with their textbook resources. As we have seen, researchers such as Gardner (e.g., 1999) have established that there are many ways of knowing and learning, not all of them involving linguistic intelligence. You may, for instance, have students who have a great deal of logical/mathematical intelligence or a great deal of visual/spatial intelligence. For these students, multimodal resources can allow them to experience the content you are teaching in ways that allow them to use their own strengths. Moreover, for students whose strength is not linguistic intelligence, supports such as within-text cues, indices, and glossaries allow them the development of stronger literacy skills.

Textbook resources can also be very beneficial for ELL students. As researchers such as Cummins (e.g., 1994) have shown, ELL students may have a great deal of content knowledge in their own language, but not in English. Non-linguistic resources such as maps and graphs help these students tap into their prior knowledge more easily, and linguistic resources such as within-text cues provide necessary scaffolds for their English language development.

Struggling readers also profit from learning to use textbook resources. These students often need assistance in organizing material they read into schemas; within-text cues provide that assistance. Headings, sub-headings, bold/italicized words, and glossed vocabulary help struggling readers organize concepts into hierarchies, separate important from less-important information, and related ideas. Tables of contents, glossaries, and indices offer extra information that the struggling reader may find difficult to learn from the text itself. Maps and other graphic cues offer alternative ways of experiencing the content, so that the struggling reader can find support for his/her developing reading comprehension skills.

THIEVES

As we have seen, students may very well not know how to use their textbook resources; alternatively, they may know how to use those resources but not understand the value of using them. So direct coaching on how to use what is available in a textbook can be a valuable use of your classroom time. One way to coach students in the use of textbook resources is a strategy called THIEVES, developed by Suzanne Manz (2002). In this strategy, students learn to preview a chapter or a section of a chapter in order to organize the chapter's information as they read it.

THIEVES is an acronym that reminds students of the places in their textbook where they will likely find information they need to understand the concepts they are learning. The teacher begins implementing this strategy by telling students they are going to learn to get into textbooks and "steal" the information from the text; in other words, they are going to be thieves. To do this, they need to learn where to look. You can adapt this introduction to meet the needs of your students and to focus on your particular content area. The main goal is that students be directly coached on how to use THIEVES. Figure 6.4 shows the elements of THIEVES and the questions you can coach students to ask themselves as they look at each resource in their textbooks.

Once students have learned where to look for the most important information in their textbooks, they can then focus their attention on those resources. This allows students to organize what they are reading and make more efficient use of their reading time. That organization also empowers students to deepen their reading comprehension, since they will already have schemas with which they can associate what they read. Finally, a strategy such as THIEVES provides students with a scaffold for active reading, whether they are reading independently or with coaching.

Figure 6.4: THIEVES and Sample Questions

T	Title	What do I already know about this topic? How is it related to previous information? What do I think this is going to be about?
H	Headings	What does this heading let me know I will be reading about? What is the topic of the paragraph beneath it? How can I turn this heading into a question that is likely to be answered in the actual content? (Manz, 2002, p. 434).
I	Introduction	Is there an opening, perhaps italicized? Does the first paragraph introduce the chapter? What does the introduction let me know I will be reading about? Do I know anything about this already? (Manz, p. 434)
E	Every first sentence in a paragraph	What important information is given that provides me with clues about the topic of the paragraph? Does the first sentence of the paragraph tell me what the topic is?
V	Visuals and vocabulary	Are there photographs, drawings, maps, charts, graphs? What can I learn from them? How do the captions help me better understand the meaning? (Manz, p. 434).
E	End-of-chapter questions	What do the questions ask? What information do they earmark as important? What information do I learn from the question? (Manz, p. 434).
S	Summary	Does the chapter end with a summary that tells me the most important points of the chapter? What are the most important points of this chapter? Is there anything that the author has omitted?

Conclusion

If students are to become active readers and make the most of their during reading time, they need to be able to organize what they are reading and associate what they read with what they know. Good readers preview a text and get a sense of what they are going to read; beginning and struggling readers may not have the skills they need to do this. So, your direct instruction and the scaffolds you provide are extremely important for those students.

As students make the transition from narrative to expository text, even good readers may need assistance in identifying and using a variety of new text structures and textbook resources. It is important not to assume that, just because a student is a fluent reader, he/she can automatically get the most from a textbook without coaching. In fact, working with your students on textbook skills is a valuable investment of class time. Strong textbook skills often translate into more efficient use of reading time, more successful independent reading, and better recall of information.

Chapter 6 Reflection

1. How is most of the content in the texts you use presented? Is it presented within the text in the form of charts, graphs, and other illustrations? What skills do your students need the most to understand the texts you use?

   _____

   _____

   _____

   _____

2. What is the structure of the text you use most often? What sorts of information does this structure provide? How do you communicate this to your students?

   _____

   _____

   _____

   _____

3. What, if any, text-reading skills do your students struggle with the most? In what direct ways might you consider coaching on these skills?

   _____

   _____

   _____

   _____

Visual Representations of Text

Thus far, we have been focusing on ways to help your students understand and process the text they read and derive meaning from the words and sentences in that text. It is important to keep in mind that using and processing text requires what Howard Gardner (e.g., 1999) terms *linguistic intelligence*. This kind of intelligence entails having a sense of words and the ways in which they work. If researchers such as Gardner are correct, then we all have a certain amount of linguistic intelligence and, thus, we can all develop our linguistic intelligence.

However, we vary greatly with respect to the extent of our various intelligences; this means that your students are likely to possess a variety of intelligences. For example, some will have strong linguistic intelligence, others will have strong logical/mathematical intelligence, and still others will have strong kinesthetic intelligence. Since not all of your students will have strong linguistic intelligence, it is very helpful to support their developing literacy skills by using a variety of ways to represent text. One of the most common and most useful alternatives for representing text is through visual means.

Visual representations of text allow those students with strong visual/spatial intelligence to use that strength to support their developing linguistic intelligence. They also allow students with strong linguistic intelligence to support their developing visual/spatial intelligence. In other words, visual representations of text serve as helpful scaffolds for the development of multiple intelligences.

There are other reasons for which you will want to integrate visual representations of text into your curriculum. One of these is that visual representations are very helpful for ELL students, who may have strong conceptual backgrounds and prior knowledge in their own language(s), but not in English (e.g., Wilson, 1999). Visuals can assist these students in making connections between their own knowledge and the English language material they are reading. Linda Hoyt (2002) includes a long list of strategies for building ELL students' content knowledge in informational texts, many of which involve utilizing visual representations of text. Some examples include having students summarize text with notes and sketches as they read or having them label pictures in books or their own illustrations with sticky notes.

Visual representations are also beneficial for struggling readers (e.g., Hibbing & Rank-Erickson, 2003). These students may have great difficulty independently creating mental imagery as they read text (Hibbing & Rank-Erickson), so seeing an illustration, chart, or other graphic can help them to construct an accurate mental portrait of what they are reading. Visuals are also useful in helping struggling readers become aware of when they have not understood the text they are reading.

Integrating the Visual Into Your Instruction

There are a variety of ways in which you can incorporate visual representations into your curriculum. We will first look at ways in which you can present visuals and help students use the visuals in their texts, and then we will turn to ways in which students themselves can learn to represent visually what they read.

Films

As Hibbing and Rank-Erickson (2003) point out, films can be very helpful in facilitating students' mental representations of text. Many novels and stories have been adapted for film or television and are available in VHS or DVD format. These adaptations can easily be borrowed or rented. Films may be especially helpful for text that can be difficult to read (e.g., J.K. Rowling's *Harry Potter and the Chamber of Secrets*).

Even if the content you are teaching is not a novel, play, or other narrative text, you can still use films to help your students better understand the text they read. Many organizations such as the National Geographic Society offer films and television series on a wide variety of topics. Using video clips, as opposed to entire videos, is also an effective strategy for illustrating concepts. The Discovery Education Network provides a subscription service to thousands of clips for educators. Incorporating these from time to time can help students build or tap into background knowledge to help them better comprehend as they are reading.

Graphic Organizers

Throughout this book, you have been reading about a variety of ways in which graphic organizers can be used to prepare your students to read and to assist them while they are reading. Graphic organizers can help students learn to categorize information they read and associate that information with what they have already learned. They can also help students recall what they have read for later use. As you read in Chapter 6, many textbooks provide graphic organizers to illustrate various concepts, and it is to your students' advantage for you to coach them in using those graphics to help them as they read. Sometimes, texts do not provide useful graphics. At other times, you may want to add graphics of your own to a lesson. In those cases, you will want a repertoire of types of organizers so that you can choose the one that will best represent the content you are teaching. Let's look at two kinds of organizers you may find useful.

One kind of organizer is the Venn diagram. These organizers are generally used to represent the relationships between sets of things. Venn diagrams originated in mathematics, but are now also used in many other content areas. Let us look at an example of how you might use a Venn diagram in your own content area.

Suppose your first-grade students are studying the differences and similarities between plants and animals. As they prepare to read a section in their textbooks about the way plants and animals get food, hand out a Venn diagram such as the one in Figure 7.1.

Post a large copy of the same diagram on the whiteboard so that students can follow your model as you explain the diagram. Tell students that they are going to read about what makes plants and animals the same and what makes them different, and that the diagram they have will make it easier for them to remember. Then, instruct your students to carefully read the passage you indicate

Figure 7.1: Sample Venn Diagram of Plants and Animals

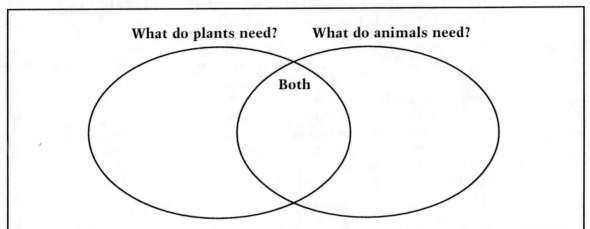

and to write down each thing they learn about plants and animals. Things that are true only of plants will go in the left circle, and things that are true only of animals will go in the right circle. Things that are true of both plants and animals will be written in the space where the circles overlap. Coach your students by reading the first sentence and filling in the first part of the Venn diagram. Then, have students work in pairs to complete the passage and fill in the rest of the diagram as they read. When students are finished with their diagrams, review the diagram with the whole class and have students look at their own diagrams to be sure that they have understood correctly what they read.

Venn diagrams are only one way to represent concepts visually. Another way in which you can use graphics to represent concepts is ***semantic webbing***, also known as ***concept webbing***. Semantic, or concept, webs are used to help organize various aspects of a concept so that the reader can associate the concept's attributes into one schema. Concept webs are flexible enough to use in nearly any content area and for many topics. For example, you might use concept webs to represent personality traits of the main character of a story or to help students remember the characteristics of reptiles.

To further help you integrate these webs into your teaching, consider this concrete illustration of the use of a concept web in a mathematics class. Suppose your second-grade students are about to read a section of their mathematics text that describes some of the various shapes they will be learning about. Since your students have already read about circles and rectangles, you want them to focus on squares. Before your students begin reading about squares, hand out a web such as the one in Figure 7.2.

Figure 7.2: Sample Semantic/Concept Web for Squares

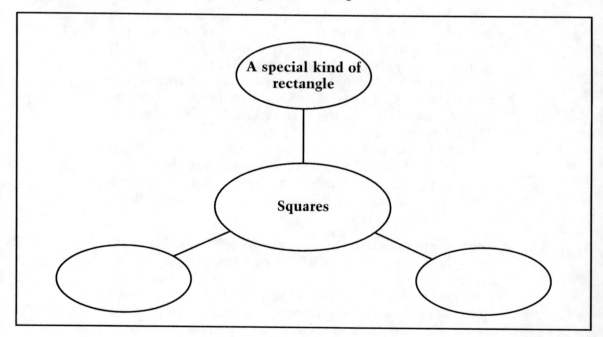

Explain to students that they will be reading about squares, and the web will help them remember what makes a square unique. Instruct students to carefully read the passage in their texts that describes squares and to write down what they learned about squares in each bubble of the diagram. Model your expectations for students by having them read the first few sentences of the passage chorally as you lead. Then say, "Here's one thing I found out about squares—they're a special kind of rectangle." Write that fact in one of the bubbles. Once you are sure that students understand what to do, have them take turns reading sentences in small groups, filling out the diagram as they read. When the groups are done reading, have one member of each group announce its findings to the class while you provide feedback. End the lesson by having the students check their own answers to be sure they have understood what they read.

Sometimes, you will want students to be able to organize what they read into chart or graph form. As an example of this kind of graphic organizer, let us consider the timeline. When students are reading about a series of events, it's helpful for them to be able to recall the order of those events so as to associate them accurately. In that case, you might want students to have a timeline to help them organize the information they are reading.

Here is an example of a way in which you might integrate a timeline to help your students read actively. Suppose your students are preparing to read about the development of China during the Middle Ages. You want them to be able to organize the information they read chronologically, so before your students read their text, hand out a timeline such as the one in Figure 7.3. Instruct your students to silently read the section of their chapter that introduces the dynasties and gives an overview of the major developments and accomplishments of each dynasty. Ask them to list on the timeline three developments they read about for each dynasty. As

Figure 7.3: Sample Timeline for the Development of Ancient China

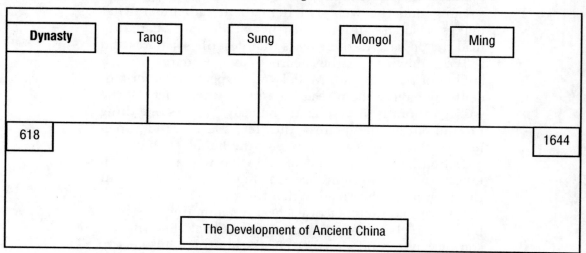

students read, walk around the room answering questions and ensuring that students understand what to do. When students are finished reading, ask individual students to go up to the whiteboard, on which you have pasted a large poster depicting the timeline, and write on the poster some of the developments they read about. Finish the lesson by having students check their own timelines for accuracy.

Student-Produced Visuals

Once students have had some experience working with visuals, they can learn to produce their own. In fact, research shows that student recall and understanding is improved when students create graphic organizers after they read (Mealy & Nist, 1989). There are several reasons for this. One is that students who create their own visuals also have the opportunity to use their visual/spatial intelligence as well as their linguistic intelligence. This means they are likely to make more and stronger associations between what they are reading and what they already know. Another reason for which student-generated visuals can be helpful has to do with schemas (see Chapter 3). We tend to have the strongest and best-developed schemas of concepts that are personally meaningful. So when a student creates his/her own graphic representation, that representation is more authentic and meaningful for the student than a mental representation that's imposed from "the outside."

Besides enhancing recall, student-created visuals have other advantages. One is that student-produced visuals provide an effective assessment tool. Students' visuals are the product of their own mental representations. So the teacher can use those visuals to find out whether students have understood what they were reading. Also, student-generated graphic representations increase students' personal investment in what they are reading. This may, in turn, increase their motivation, which, as researchers such as Skinner and Belmont (1993) argue, may increase the amount of time in which students are actively involved with the content they are learning.

Integrating student-produced visuals into your curriculum is, as you have seen, beneficial for students; it is also fairly easy and can be adapted for a variety of grade levels. As an example, consider this scenario. Your first-grade students are working on their addition and subtraction facts. You want to be sure that they understand the concept of what it means to add and subtract, so you give each student a handout such as the one in Figure 7.4 and place your own copy of the handout on the overhead projector.

Explain to the class that they have already learned that numbers tell a story. Now you want them to draw pictures that go with number stories. Model your expectations for your students by calling their attention to the overhead projector. Read the first addition fact and remind your students that the story tells about five of

Figure 7.4: Sample Student-Generated Graphic Organizer for Addition and Subtraction

something added to one of something and that the end of the story is six of that something. Then, use a think-aloud protocol (see Chapter 4) to work through the problem and draw a series of pictures, explaining what you are doing as you go along. When you are done drawing, use another think-aloud strategy to count the number of pictures you have drawn and compare those numbers to the corresponding numerals. Then, ask students to work with buddies and draw pictures that show the same thing as each number story they see on their paper, just as you did. As students pair up and begin to work, walk around the room to be certain that everyone understands what to do and that students are able to complete the task. When students are done with their illustrations, invite them to go up to the overhead projector and draw their pictures on the transparency you have left there. The lesson ends as students check their own work by counting the objects in their pictures to compare those objects to their corresponding numerals.

As students move through the grade levels, their visuals can become more self-initiated, more detailed, and more sophisticated. You will find that the role student-created visuals play in your content teaching will depend in part on the grade level you are teaching as well as on the experience your students have with creating their own graphics.

A Note About Technology

Today's technology allows for more integration of the visual into your instruction than ever before. Computer software such as PowerPoint, Inspiration, and other graphics creation programs allow you and your students to create visuals from simple sketches and line drawings to fully animated stories that include music or voice-over technology. These advances in technology can empower you to enhance your instruction and make it more accessible to your students. They also empower your students to express themselves and demonstrate their understanding in a wide variety of ways.

Because of the learning potential inherent in technology, it is to your benefit (and to that of your students) to be familiar with a variety of technology tools. The more familiar you are with the choices technology offers, the better able you will be to select the most appropriate tools for the content you are teaching. Moreover, nearly 62 percent of U.S. households now have home computers (U.S. Census Bureau, 2005). So, chances are that your students will come to your classroom with some knowledge about computers, and perhaps experience working with software. Tapping into that prior knowledge can be very helpful as you integrate literacy skills into your content.

Conclusion

Since today's students come from a wide variety of backgrounds and linguistic and literacy experiences, it is important to use as many ways as possible to present concepts. One of the most powerful ways to represent the concepts you are teaching is through visual means. Visuals can take many forms, from simple sketches to full-length films. They can include technology aids and can be produced by you, your students, or all of you working together.

Visuals are powerful because they allow students to develop strong mental representations of the content you are teaching; these representations don't have to depend solely on students' linguistic intelligence. Visuals therefore serve as scaffolds for students who are developing their linguistic and literacy skills. They also serve as scaffolds for students with strong linguistic intelligence who are developing their visual/spatial intelligence. Visuals also provide a means for students to connect their own real-world knowledge to the material they are reading.

Your choice of which visuals to use and how to integrate them will depend on your content, your students' age and ability levels, and your goals. So, it is to your advantage, and to that of your students, to become thoroughly familiar with a variety of visual ways to represent your content and to coach your students in doing so. It is also to everyone's benefit to coach your students in using the visual supports to which they have access (e.g., textbook graphics, classroom maps and globes, and handouts you provide). Once students become familiar with using these tools, they will be better able to create them themselves and to use them as learning supports.

Chapter 7 Reflection

1. What technology resources are easily available to you? To what extent do you use them to represent content visually?

   _____

   _____

   _____

   _____

2. Consider the content you most often teach. Which sort of graphic organizer best depicts the major concepts within that content?

   _____

   _____

   _____

   _____

3. Examine a textbook that you use frequently. What visual supports does the textbook contain? To what extent are your students familiar with those supports and ways to use them?

   _____

   _____

   _____

   _____

PHASE III: POST-READING

- Summarizing
- Questioning

Summarizing

Up to this point, we have been focusing on ways to pre-pare your students to read and ways to help them derive meaning from text while they are reading. As you read in Chapter 1, these pre- and during-reading activities are important for successful overall reading comprehension. In the next two chapters of this book, we will turn our attention to the last phase of the three-phase model we have been assuming: the post-reading phase. You will recall from Chapter 1 that post-reading activities help readers extend their learning and apply what they have read; they also help readers associate what they have read with what they already know.

Strategies for Teaching Summarization

There are several approaches you can take to provide your students with post-reading experiences. The first approach we will discuss is summarizing. Summarization has several benefits; one of them is that it focuses the readers on the major points of a text and helps them to eliminate what is less important. Through summarization, the reader can also review a text and organize what he/she has read (Kim, 2002). Research shows that coaching students in summarization strategies helps them to remember what they read longer. For instance, Malone and Mastropieri (1991) studied three groups of students. One group was taught via traditional reading comprehension approaches, another was taught via summarization strategies, and the third was taught via summarization and self-monitoring strategies. Malone and Mastropieri found that both groups of students who were taught to summarize outperformed the group that was not taught to summarize.

Summarization can be taught at a wide variety of grade levels and in all content areas. Let us now look at a few strategies you can use to teach your students how to summarize.

GIST (Generating Interactions Between Schemata and Text)

GIST was developed by James Cunningham (1982) as a strategy for helping students to learn how to pick out the most important information from a text. This strategy begins with the teacher selecting a passage from a text students will be reading. Once this passage has been chosen, the teacher explains to the students that they will be learning a strategy for getting the most important details from what they read. The teacher then places 15 lines on the overhead or whiteboard and instructs students to read the first sentence of the passage. The students are told to summarize that sentence using no more than 15 words which correspond to the 15 available lines. Once this task is completed, students are asked to read the second sentence and revise the summary the class is developing, so that the summary of the two sentences is no more than 15 words. Students continue reading the passage, revising their class summary after each sentence. In this way, students end up with a 15-word summary of an entire passage. After the teacher leads the whole class in their initial GIST experience, students can then use this strategy in small groups and later individually.

As you experiment with GIST, you will find that it can be adapted for content and grade level. For instance, GIST can be used to solve word problems in mathematics (Lester, Head, Elliott, Simoneaux, & Trowbridge, 2001). In this version, as in other versions, the teacher begins by selecting a word problem and guiding the whole class in using the strategy. After students are oriented to the task, they are asked to read a word problem and select the 12 most important words needed to solve the problem. Later, when they have some experience, students can use this version of GIST to solve word problems in small groups or individually.

To get a sense of how GIST might be implemented in your classroom, consider this example. Your fifth-grade students are learning about the properties of elements; specifically, they are about to read a section of their text that describes atoms and their components. Before your students read this passage, announce that students are going to learn to summarize what they read so that they can remember it better. Then hand out a chart such as the one in Figure 8.1 to each student and place your own copy of this chart on the overhead projector.

Figure 8.1: Sample of GIST

What are the most important things to remember about this section on elements?

All elements are made of atoms (protons, neutrons, electrons). Molecules have more than one atom.

Tell the students that you are all going to be reading the passage together. Have a student read the first sentence. After that sentence is read, stop the class and ask the students what the most important point in that sentence is. Then, model for students how to place those words on the lines you have provided in their handouts. Have another student read the next sentence and again ask students for the most important points. This time, students tell you which words to place on the blank lines. As you and the students go through the passage together, revise the words on the lines after each sentence. When you have finished the passage, you should have a 15-word summary of the entire passage (see Figure 8.1). When the summary is finished, tell your students that they now have a handy review sheet that they can later use to remember what they read. Now that your students have been introduced to GIST, you can coach them on using this strategy in their small groups and later, as an individual study strategy.

Four-Two-One

Like GIST, Four-Two-One is designed to help students focus on the most important information they read and leave out what is less important. This strategy begins with the teacher asking students to think of four words that best reflect what they have learned. Then, students share their lists of words either in pairs or small groups and develop a set of words they have in common. From this list, students distill two words that they agree capture the most important points. Finally, the pair or team of students chooses one word or main idea that reflects the main point they have learned. As a closing activity, pairs or teams share their choices with the rest of the class (Rogers, Ludington, & Graham, 1999).

Part of the appeal of Four-Two-One is that it is an easy and flexible strategy that requires little preparation on your part. It is also a strategy that students can use independently after they have learned how to apply it. Let us now look at an example of how you can implement Four-Two-One in your class. Suppose your students are learning about communities of populations and how those communities interact. Your students have just finished reading a section in their texts that describes the roles that producers, consumers, and decomposers play in the interactions between populations. You want to be certain that students have understood the main points of the passages they read, so you announce to the class that you are going to show them a way to remember the main points of what they read. Ask each student to list on a sheet of paper four words that capture the passage's main points. When students have finished their lists, have them turn to a partner and share their lists and then develop a list of two words that best reflect the passage's meaning. After the pairs have completed this task, have them choose one of those two words as their main idea. The activity ends as each pair shares its idea. An example of how these words might look can be seen in Figure 8.2.

Figure 8.2: Sample Four-Two-One in a Life Science Class

Gina	Roberto
Populations	Producers
Consumers	Interaction
Producers	Consumers
Interaction	Populations
Gina and Roberto's words	
Populations	Interaction
Gina and Roberto's final word: Interaction	

Once students understand how to use one or two words to capture the main points of passages that they read, they can keep those words or phrases in a journal or notebook as guides for independent studying. These words or phrases can also be used to compile personal glossaries for students to use to help build their vocabularies. Additional follow-up activities might include using graphic organizers (see Chapter 7) to develop students' conceptual frameworks or having students use the ideas they generate during Four-Two-One to write their own summaries of passages they read.

Direct Instruction of Summarization Strategies

Another approach to teaching students how to summarize is through direct instruction. As we have seen, direct instruction is efficient and allows the teacher to quickly assess students' ability to use the skill they are learning. While direct instruction is neither necessary nor appropriate for all of the skills you will be teaching, it is a legitimate alternative in many cases. Let us now consider how summarization might be taught through explicit instruction.

Brown, Campione, and Day (1981) developed four rules for summarizing: 1) Delete trivial material that is unnecessary to understanding; 2) Delete redundant material; 3) Substitute superordinate terms (*flowers* for *daisies, tulips,* and *roses*); 4) Select a topic sentence or invent one. To help your students learn to use these rules when they read, you might consider presenting them to your whole class and then directly coaching the class in their use. Marzano, Pickering, and Pollock (2001) suggest using a modeling strategy such as think-aloud (see Chapter 4) to show students how to use these rules.

Here is an illustration of how you might use a think-aloud strategy to coach your students on using Brown,

Campione, and Day's rules. Your fifth-grade students are reading about the events of the American Revolution. They have finished reading the section of their chapter that explains Patrick Henry's role in the Revolutionary War and the significance of his "No Taxation Without Representation" speech. You want your students to summarize this section of the chapter, so you explain to the class that as their reading gets more complicated, they are going to want a way to separate what is important from what is less important as they read. Give each student a copy of Brown, Campione, and Day's four rules for summarizing. After briefly mentioning each rule, tell your students that you are going to show them an example of how to use those rules. Place a transparency of part of the section your students have just read on the overhead projector. Then, begin to read that section aloud. As you read, stop from time to time and think-aloud (e.g., "Okay, this section is about taxation enforced by the British Parliament on the American colonists . . . there's the definition of taxation, and I need that, so I'll write it down. This next part is just an example of the taxation imposed on the colonists, so I'm going to just write the word and the definition; I don't need a lot of examples. This last sentence just repeats the first part of the paragraph, so I don't need to put that in my notes, either. Now all I need is a topic sentence or idea—I'll just use 'taxation' as my topic."). Once you have given this example to students, have them silently read the next section of their texts, using the rules you have taught as they read. When students are finished reading, ask them to share their summaries with a partner and compare notes. Have each pair share its summary with the rest of the class.

Conclusion

Whether you decide to use direct instruction or some other approach, it is important to show students how to summarize what they have read. Summarization allows students to focus on the main points of a passage. It also helps students connect what they read with their existing schemas. Finally, summarization provides students with a resource to use as they study independently and serves to organize their prior knowledge for further reading.

Besides the benefits to students, summarization is also useful for the teacher. Many teachers use summaries as an assessment tool; by reading student summaries, the teacher can see whether students have noticed and remembered the main points of the text they read. Summaries also provide the teacher with information about students' mental representations of text. The ways in which students organize information in their summaries is very likely a reflection of the ways in which they organize that information in their minds. Some teachers even use student summaries as a resource for study guides, test questions, and other learning materials.

Chapter 8 Reflection

1. Choose a section from a textbook you use frequently. What are the main points your students need to remember from that section? What words or phrases best capture those points?

   _____

   _____

   _____

   _____

2. Select and read a journal article that you find interesting. As you read it, pay attention to the strategies you use to summarize the information you read. How do those strategies help you connect that information with what you already know?

   _____

   _____

   _____

   _____

3. In what ways do you get information about your students' mental representations of what they read? How might student summaries fit into your approach for connecting with your students' schemas?

   _____

   _____

   _____

   _____

Questioning

The most frequently used technique that teachers use to assess and develop student understanding is the use of questions (Ryder & Graves, 2003). In fact, a great deal of the dialogue that typically goes on in a classroom is couched in the form of questions and answers. In this chapter, we will take a close look at questions and ways in which you and your students can use well-developed questions to promote greater comprehension of what students read.

As we will see shortly, questions vary greatly. Some require a great deal of high-level thought; others can be answered quickly with only a word or two. So, one important skill you will want to develop is the ability to integrate questions at a wide variety of levels into your curriculum. You will also want to integrate several opportunities for your students to generate and answer their own questions. This sort of questioning allows students to set a purpose for their reading (see Chapter 5). Having students develop their own questions also helps increase their motivation, since they are likely to be actively engaged in answering questions they themselves have posed. Let us now take a close look at the kinds of questions you can use to enhance comprehension, and ways in which you can implement questioning techniques in your content area.

What Kinds of Questions Do We Ask?

One of the most famous and widely used comprehension hierarchies is Bloom's Taxonomy (Bloom, 1984). This taxonomy categorizes questions based on the level of understanding and cognitive engagement required to answer them. As you can see in Figure 9.1, questions that are lower on the taxonomy (i.e., Knowledge) require less engagement, while higher-level questions (i.e., Evaluation) require more engagement.

Figure 9.1: Bloom's Taxonomy of Questions

	Defining Characteristics	Example Questions
1. Knowledge	Simple recall of facts or information	"What is the capital of Argentina?"
2. Comprehension	Understanding the meaning of those facts or information	"Describe the character of Othello."
3. Application	Using information in new situations	"Use the FOIL method to simplify the following expressions."
4. Analysis	Breaking down concepts into their components and using those components to compare and contrast ideas; drawing inferences and making predictions	"Look at the litmus paper you've used in this experiment. What does it tell you about the 'mystery liquid' you just tested? How do you know?"
5. Synthesis	Using prior knowledge to create something new or different	"We've been reading about overpopulation in certain parts of the world. What are your ideas for solving the overpopulation problem? Be prepared to defend your suggestions."
6. Evaluation	Making judgments about the value of facts, ideas, or concepts based on one's knowledge of those concepts	"Did Harry Truman make the right decision to authorize the use of the atomic bomb? Take a position on this question and support your position."

One of the interesting phenomena about questioning in the classroom is that most questions tend to be lower-level questions (Alvermann & Hayes, 1989). The problem with only focusing on lower-level questions is that this strategy doesn't allow your students to interact with the material you are teaching as much as they can when you vary the type of questions you and your students ask. So, the emphasis in this chapter is on integrating a variety of types of questions into your repertoire of teaching strategies. We will begin with questions that you might pose and ways to pose them effectively; then we will take up the topic of student-generated questions.

Teacher-Generated Questions

When most people think of questions in the classroom, they often think of questions that the teacher asks and students answer; after all, this is one the most common ways in which teachers find out what their students know (Ryder & Graves, 2003). So it shouldn't be surprising to learn that the way in which you form and pose questions plays an important role in your students' ability to learn from them. Let us consider some ways in which you can modify your questions so as to help students make the most of this strategy.

Levels of Questions

One way in which you can make the most of asking questions is to vary the cognitive demand that they place on your students. As we have seen, the cognitive level of a question is an important consideration. If you review Figure 9.1, you will see that each level in Bloom's Taxonomy requires more engagement with the material and more investment of one's own prior knowledge than the previous level. So, when you ask your students more complex questions as well as lower-level ones, you are giving them opportunities to interact at sophisticated levels with the material they are learning.

Higher-level questions also provide the teacher with the opportunity to assess student understanding of a topic. Suppose, for instance, that your students are learning about the Pythagorean Theorem. Asking your students what the Pythagorean Theorem is will only give you information about whether they know that formula; it won't let you know whether your students understand how to use it. In this case, you would want to ask a question at a higher level of demand, e.g., "How would you use the Pythagorean Theorem to solve this word problem?"

A Note About Wait-Time

As you think about the cognitive level of the questions you ask, you will also want to consider wait-time. In this context, wait-time refers to the amount of time a teacher allows between asking a question and expecting a student to respond. Research shows that the typical wait-time teachers allow is only one second (Hornea, 1982). One second may give students enough time to answer a knowledge-level question (see Figure 9.1), but does not provide enough time for students to answer a more complex question at a higher level.

The upshot of the research on wait-time is that when teachers wait longer after they ask questions, students are more likely to be able to answer them in a meaningful way. Increasing wait-time doesn't necessarily mean you have to wait indefinitely for an answer. In fact, Hornea (1982) found that increasing wait-time by just a few seconds also increased students' ability to answer a variety of questions at different levels of cognitive demand.

Sequencing of Questions

Teachers can also enhance their questioning skills by considering the order in which they pose questions. If you plan the sequence of questions you ask about what students read, you can also guide them towards a deeper processing of the material (Ryder & Graves, 2003). The effective teacher sequences questions by first choosing the goal of the questions, so that each question contributes to that goal. Then the teacher identifies the information that students will need to reach that goal and constructs questions that address that information. Ultimately, the goal is addressed in a high-level question, and lower-level questions are used to highlight information that the student will need to respond to the higher-level questions (Ryder & Graves).

Questioning the Author (QtA)

Sometimes, rather than simply presenting questions in a whole-class situation, you will want students to use questions as guides while they are reading. This strategy, developed by Beck, McKeown, Hamilton, and Kucon (1997), is designed to promote greater comprehension of text in just such a situation. QtA begins with the teacher carefully reviewing a text that students will be reading and selecting important ideas and concepts. Then, the teacher generates questions and themes that are based on those concepts. Once the overarching themes, ideas, and questions have been developed, the teacher breaks down the larger reading into smaller segments that are associated with a limited number of questions, so that students will only be reading a short segment at a time. After this planning is completed, the teacher introduces QtA to the students, telling them that they will be reading and discussing a set of passages. Since these passages are the written form of someone's words, they can best be understood through discussion. Once students understand what to do, the teacher divides the students into groups, and each group reads the first passage and discusses its meaning, using the questions the teacher provides. When those questions are answered, the group moves on to the next passage. Here are some examples of questions that might be posed as students are discussing text:

1. What is the author's message here?
2. What is the author trying to say?
3. Why did the author give that detail here?
4. What do you think the author meant by that?

QtA allows students to interact with a text and engage in active reading in an organized way. QtA also offers students a model for posing their own questions as they read independently.

Here is an example of how you might implement QtA in your own class. Suppose your students are reading about nutrition and healthy eating habits. In order to add to their reading experience, provide your students with a short article by a doctor that describes the USDA food pyramid and the importance of its categories. Explain to your students that they will be reading a very short article about the food pyramid and that they will need to keep in mind that this article is being told by a person with a particular point of view. In order for them to really understand what that person is saying, they will need to discuss what they read. Then, break students into groups of four and hand each group a set of questions, such as the ones below. You should also place these questions on the whiteboard for later use:

1. What does the author tell us about the food pyramid?
2 Why does the author tell us those particular facts?
3. What did the author mean by "nutritional requirements"?
4. What do you think the author regards as the food pyramid's greates value? Why?

Next, instruct students to begin reading the first passage of the article. After they have read the first passage, have students discuss it, focusing their conversation on the questions you have provided. As students engage in their discussions, walk around the room, ensuring that everyone understands what to do and monitoring students' conversations to check on their comprehension of the text. After all of the groups have finished answering the questions, have a representative of each group come up to the whiteboard and write that group's responses to the questions. The activity ends with the students checking their answers.

Question/Answer Relationships (QAR)

This strategy is designed to help students learn how to use their texts to answer a variety of different questions at different levels. Answers to some questions can be found directly within a text; these are ***text-explicit*** questions. The answers to other questions require skills such as summarizing, classifying, organizing, and putting concepts together; these questions are ***text-implicit***. Finally, some questions require students to hypothesize, predict, or infer; these high-level questions are ***script-implicit*** questions. To illustrate these types of questions clearly, consider these sample questions from Roald Dahl's *Charlie and the Chocolate Factory*:

1. Who lives in Charlie Bucket's house? (text-explicit)

2. What is Charlie's favorite food? (text-explicit)

3. Is Charlie's family well-to-do or poor? How do you know? (text-implicit)

4. Why does Charlie love chocolate so much? (text-implicit)

5. How do you think Charlie dresses? Why? (script-implicit)

6. Where do you think Charlie's town is located? How do you know? (script-implicit)

In order to help students use their texts effectively to answer these types of questions, the teacher begins QAR by letting students know that there are three places to look for answers to questions they have about what they read. One place is right in the text (a text-explicit question); this type of question is called a "Right There" question. Other kinds of answers are in the text, too, only it takes a little searching and thinking to find the answer (text-implicit question); those are called "Think and Search" questions. Finally, some answers require some thinking on the student's own part (script-implicit questions); those answers aren't found in the text. Those questions are called "In My Head" questions.

Once the students are clear about the three places to look for answers to questions, the teacher provides students with some questions about a text they are about to read. The teacher asks students to categorize those questions according to where they might look for an answer. Students would then begin to read, answering the questions as they go along. After the reading, the teacher debriefs the students, getting their input as to where they found the information to answer the questions.

To illustrate QAR more fully, let us return to *Charlie and the Chocolate Factory*. Your third-grade students are about to begin the book, and you would like them to engage in active reading. You begin the lesson by telling your students that they are going to learn a way to look in the right places for answers as they read, so they can be better "reading detectives." You then give each student a handout such as the one in Figure 9.2, with plenty of room below for writing examples of each type of question for future reference.

After briefly reviewing the handout, ask students to write in their journals questions you have designed about the first chapter of the novel and have written on the whiteboard (for a sample set of questions, see the questions for *Charlie and the Chocolate Factory* at the bottom of page 117). Have volunteer students tell you which QAR category they would use to answer each question. Once your students have written the questions in their journals, ask them to begin reading and to answer the questions as they read. When students are finished with the first few passages, have them share their answers in small groups. End the lesson by having each group present its answers to the class.

Figure 9.2: Sample QAR Guide

Right There	Think and Search	In My Head
Words and sentences that I read will answer the question.	What's written in the text combined with what I already know will answer the question.	Only my own ideas will answer the question.

Student-Generated Questions

In order for students to actively process what they read, you will want them to be able to create their own questions. Creating one's own questions taps into prior knowledge, motivates the reader to satisfy his/her curiosity, and provides an important purpose for reading. Questions also serve to organize one's reading.

There are several strategies you can use to coach your students to ask useful questions and look for the answers in the text they read. One strategy, for instance, is the use of the KWL Chart (see Chapter 3). You will recall from Chapter 3 that one component of the KWL Chart is a set of questions that students pose after they have considered what they already know about a topic. These student-generated questions help students focus as they read and note important information that leads them toward answers to their questions. Let us now look at two other strategies for helping students pose helpful questions.

Write a Question

This is a quick and easy strategy for teaching students to generate their own questions. This strategy, adapted from Middendorf and Kalish (1996), is designed to make lectures more meaningful for students by integrating activities that engage students. In Write a Question, the teacher asks the students to write down a question they have about the topic at hand. Students then share their questions with a partner, small group, or the whole class. Then, the students can read the selected text, searching for the answer to their question as they read.

For instance, suppose your sixth-grade students are learning about thermal energy. You prepare a demonstration to show how heat flows from warmer objects to cooler objects and explain the process to the class as you demonstrate. Now that your students have the background information they need to understand the text, ask each student to write a question that he/she has about thermal energy. Then, ask students to share their questions with a partner. After students have shared their questions, have them read the passage in their text that explains thermal energy while you walk around the room to ensure that students understand what to do and to answer any questions. When students have finished reading the passage you have assigned, ask student volunteers to write their questions and the answers they found on the whiteboard. The activity ends as your students write in their journals at least one other question and its answer.

Reciprocal Questioning (ReQuest)

ReQuest was developed by Manzo (1969) as a way to help students use questions to engage more fully in what they read. Since its origin, ReQuest has been updated and modified; now ReQuest is implemented in a variety of ways. One of the most common ways involves the following steps:

1. The students and teacher begin reading a passage (this can be done either silently or aloud, with members of the class taking turns reading).

2. After the first sentence or two (depending upon students' grade level and reading ability), students ask the teacher a question about the reading, which the teacher answers.

3. The teacher answers the question and then poses one of his/her own, which the students answer.

4. Everyone continues reading the next part of the passage; the reading is followed by students and teacher again exchanging questions and answers.

After the students become comfortable with this procedure, the class can read longer passages before asking and answering questions. Later, students can ask and answer their questions within small groups (King, 1990).

Let us now look at an example of a way in which you might implement ReQuest in your classroom. Suppose your sixth-grade social studies students are learning about Ancient Greece. They are about to read a section of their textbook that describes Alexander the Great and his conquests, rule, and early death. Begin class by letting students know that they are going to be reading about Alexander the Great and that they are going to be using questions and answers to help them remember what they read. Then, ask your students to read the first few sentences of the passage silently. Also instruct them to be ready to ask you a question when they are done reading; have them to write their questions down if they would like to do so. As students are reading, walk around the room to ensure that students are focusing on what they read. When students are done reading, the following kind of exchange may take place:

Teacher: Okay, who would like to stump me with a question?

Student A: I have a question. It says here that Aristotle was Alexander the Great's teacher, but I don't remember who Aristotle was. Didn't we read about him before?

Teacher: That's right. Remember last week we were reading about Greek philosophers? Aristotle was one of them.

Student A: Oh, yeah, wasn't he Plato's student?

Teacher: Exactly, good memory! Okay, now it's my turn to ask a question. Who can give me one reason why Alexander the Great became so powerful?

Student B: I can. He had the military forces behind him. As long as they backed him up, he had power.

Teacher: That makes a lot of sense to me. Let's keep on reading and see if you're right.

You and your class then continue reading the passage, pausing after the next few sentences to exchange further questions and answers. As you can see, ReQuest allows students to practice generating their own questions with the teacher's guidance. It also permits the teacher to assess students' understanding of the passage. Finally, ReQuest provides a scaffold, in that students can use the teacher's questions and answers as a model for their own.

Conclusion

Questions serve a wide and important variety of purposes in instruction. They help students tap into their prior knowledge, they allow you to assess students' understanding of the topic, and they provide students with a purpose for reading. Questions also help structure reading, so that students can focus on the most important points in a text. Finally, questions allow students to derive meaning for themselves from a text, especially if they are student-generated questions.

As you develop questions and teach your students to do so, you will want to keep several things in mind. First, you will want to make sure that the questions you ask are at a variety of levels, so that students can engage with the material at high cognitive levels. You will also want to sequence your questions effectively, so that students have the background they need to answer higher-level questions. Finally, it's important to allow students enough time to answer questions, whether they do so verbally or in writing.

Chapter 9 Reflection

1. Choose a textbook that you frequently use. Read a passage and develop three questions that you have about the topic.

   _____

   _____

   _____

   _____

2. As you consider your response to Question 1, think about the level of questions you asked yourself. Were your questions at the same or different levels of cognitive difficulty?

   _____

   _____

   _____

   _____

3. Using the same text you used for Question 1, choose another passage, preferably one you haven't read or haven't read recently. Before reading the passage, glance at the topic and then write two questions you have. Read the passage and answer those questions. How did developing your own questions affect your reading?

   _____

   _____

   _____

   _____

Writing in the Content Areas

Up to this point, we have been focusing on literacy as it is most commonly conceived: the ability to derive meaning from reading. Yet, literacy involves a great deal more than simply reading. As we will see in this chapter, being literate also requires the ability to write. As Ryder and Graves (2003) point out, "By writing, students often find out what they know about a topic or what they want to say about it" (p. 265). In fact, Ryder and Graves (p. 266) have cited several benefits to students being able to write well:

- Writing provides the opportunity for students to interact with the material they are learning.

- Writing provides the opportunity for students to become personally involved with the text.

- Writing provides the opportunity to use students' background knowledge and experiences to make sense of the ideas and information they encounter in classes.

- Writing provides the opportunity for students to engage in meaningful communication about the ideas and information they encounter in classes.

Since writing is such an important aspect of literacy development, it is important to integrate writing practice throughout your curriculum. Not only does this integration allow students more opportunities to practice writing, but integrating writing throughout your content also enables students to use writing in authentic ways. In other words, this kind of integration provides a context for writing.

General Suggestions for Creating a "Writing-Friendly" Atmosphere

In the next section of this chapter, we will look at some specific strategies that you can use to integrate writing practice into your curriculum. First, though, let us consider some general suggestions for creating a classroom atmosphere that's conducive to writing. When your classroom atmosphere and activities encourage writing, students are more likely to take the time and make the effort to write.

Your students aren't likely to write very often if they find the writing process to be intimidating or threatening. Therefore, you will want to offer them plenty of opportunities for low-stakes (ungraded) writing (McKeatchie, 1999). In this way, students will have the chance to express themselves and become comfortable with the writing process in a nonthreatening atmosphere. They will also get more writing practice. Some examples of this kind of writing are in-class writing assignments, journaling (which we will discuss in more detail shortly), and free writing as a class warm-up activity.

Besides providing students with low-stakes writing assignments, it is also important to make sure that the writing your students do is focused on the content you are teaching rather than only the form that writing takes. Research on students' writing suggests strongly that allowing students to freely explore ideas and express themselves enables them to derive more meaning from the content they are learning and helps them use what they write to make connections to their prior knowledge (Hillocks, 2005).

Time is another important consideration in creating a "writing-friendly" environment. If students are to respond in writing and create their own written products, they need time to do so. Even writing as informal as a journal entry requires that students take the time to think and reflect before they write. It's important to set aside writing time on a regular basis. It is especially beneficial for students to have time when they are creating longer and more formal written work such as research papers or projects. As we will see, the writing process involves revision of one's original ideas, which takes time. Building plenty of time for projects into your plans helps students work more productively and ultimately, create a product of which they can be proud.

Finally, publishing student work is an integral part of teaching students to express themselves in writing. As Bromley and Mannix (1993) point out, publishing student writing helps students engage in communicating with an audience. Publishing also often serves as a strong motivator for writing; seeing one's work "in print" can be exciting and appealing. Publishing student work can be as simple as posting student essays in your classroom or as formal as submitting student work to magazines or newspapers that accept young people's writing.

The Writing Process

It takes time to produce a written expression of one's ideas. In general, the more formal and lengthy that expression, the more time is required. Let us now take a brief look at the process through which ideas take written form.

Prewriting

Many students think that they should begin to write by picking up a pencil or sitting at a keyboard. However, before writing even begins, it's important to allow students time to think about what they want to write about. Or you may wish to announce the writing topic, if you are assigning it, and then have students offer the first ideas that come to mind. Those ideas can be written on the whiteboard or taken down in students' notes, and later used as resources when students begin to write. Alternatively, you may wish to have your students write their own ideas for topics once they know the general theme of what they will write. Whichever approach you use, it's important to not neglect the idea-generation phase of writing.

Drafts

Once students have ideas about what to write, the next stage is to begin writing. Here, the emphasis should be on content, not on form (Ryder & Graves, 2003). The important goal here is for ideas to be expressed in writing, not to have everything written perfectly.

Revision

After students have drafted what they want to write, the next step is revising. Here, it's important to remember the focus on content rather than grammatical accuracy. Many teachers have students read their work to a peer; others conference with students themselves. The idea is for students to share their work with at least one other person and get constructive suggestions for revising ideas and improving the content.

Editing

In this stage of the writing process, students refine their ideas and review their work to make spelling, grammar, and other surface-level changes. Separating the editing from the revision process allows students to focus first on content and emphasize solid ideas when they write (Ryder & Graves, 2003). As students edit, they can make use of dictionaries, spelling-correction software, and other tools to make their writing more accurate. The key here is that students realize that the content of their writing is the priority; accuracy comes later.

Publishing

It's easy to forget this phase of writing, but it's an important aspect of the process. As mentioned above, when students see their writing posted in the classroom, printed in a newsletter, or published in a children's magazine, they can see themselves as authors. This vision can motivate them to write more often. So, it's in your students' interests to see their writing displayed in some lasting form.

Strategies for Integrating Writing Practice

Once you have laid the groundwork in your classroom for "user-friendly" writing, you will also want to integrate specific strategies for giving students writing practice. Ultimately, the strategies that you select will depend on your content, your students' ages and ability levels, and the purposes you and your students set for writing. What follows are only some of the available strategies for integrating writing practice. These are suggestions for strategies that can be integrated at a wide variety of grade levels and for a wide variety of content areas and purposes.

Journaling

When students have regular opportunities for journaling and other in-class writing, their attitudes towards writing tend to improve, and they write more frequently (Gau, Hermanson, Logar, & Smerek, 2003). Journaling is nonthreatening because it is not graded; therefore, students are less likely to be intimidated by the prospect of this kind of writing. ELL students and struggling writers benefit from journaling because this activity gives them needed practice in a low-stakes context. Journaling can take many forms and can be adapted for many different content areas and time structures.

Besides benefiting students, journaling also helps teachers. Journals provide the teacher with useful information about students' mental representations, so they serve as a helpful assessment tool. Journals also provide an opportunity for regular communication with students who might be reluctant to speak out in class. Finally, journals serve as a tool for both teacher and student for tracing the development of student thinking.

Let us now look at two concrete examples of ways in which you might use journaling in your classroom. Suppose your students are studying the effects of regular exercise on cardiovascular health. Your students have learned to measure their own heart rate and have read the section of their text that explains the relationship between heart rate and exercise, and you want them to derive personal meaning from this reading. Ask your students to begin by choosing some activity they like to do (e.g., walking, running, swimming, basketball, dance). Then ask them to begin an exercise log in their journals with a short paragraph in which they identify the activity they have chosen and explain their choice. Next, instruct your students to write at least two or three sentences every day that contain the following information: measured heart rate before exercise; amount and type of exercise; measured heart rate after exercise. During the following week, give your students five to ten minutes during each class session to update their journals. At the end of the week, assign your students to small groups. Each group shares its findings and draws a conclusion about the effect on group members of regular exercise on their heart rates. The groups then share their conclusions with the rest of the class.

Sometimes, journals can be used as a form of personal communication between teacher and students. Suppose, for instance, that your students are studying the U.S. Bill of Rights. They have read the section of their text that outlines what those rights are, and they have read the text of the Bill of Rights. You would like them to reflect on ways in which their own lives are affected by those rights. Have your students begin a dialogue journal by choosing the right that is most important to them. As a scaffold for this activity, provide your students with a handout listing the rights protected by the first ten amendments. Then ask students to explain in a sentence or two what their most important right is and why they believe it's important. At the beginning of the next class, collect your students' journals and respond briefly to each entry (see Figure 10.1 for a sample response). Return the journals to your students. During the next class period, give students ten minutes to respond to what you have written and then have them hand their journals back to you for your response.

Dialogue journals can be maintained over a long period of time or limited to one unit of study. They offer teacher and students the opportunity to discuss the topic at hand in a nonthreatening way that permits ongoing communication. They also allow students to make regular connections between what they are learning and their own lives.

Figure 10.1: Sample Dialogue Journal

> **Student Entry:** I think the most important right is freedom of speech. If I want to say something, I should be able to say it if it doesn't hurt anyone.
>
> **Teacher's Response:** Are there times when you think your freedom of speech is restricted?
>
> **Student's Response:** Yes. Whenever I'm talking to someone in class and you tell me to be quiet and pay attention.
>
> **Teacher's Response:** What about other students' right to listen, learn, and work?

Language Experience

In Chapter 3, you read about the importance of developing and tapping into prior knowledge when students read. One way in which you can help your students build prior knowledge is through carefully designed classroom activities that help them derive meaning from what they read. Writing can be an important part of these activities. One way in which you can use writing to help build your students' prior knowledge is through Language Experience activities, first outlined by Strickland (1969). The goal of Language Experience writing is to use students' own words to tell a story, relate an experience, or discuss a concept. In Language Experience, the teacher opens up a topic of discussion, and as students respond to the topic, the teacher writes exactly what the students say. Later, this student input can be published, handed out in printed form for review, or posted in the classroom. Language Experience can be implemented at nearly any grade level, and it can be used to review material, discuss a shared experience such as a field trip, or narrate personal anecdotes that are relevant to the topic of current study.

To get a sense of how Language Experience might be implemented in your classroom, consider the following scenario. Your first-grade students are learning to measure and compare the sizes of objects. To introduce this topic, announce that you are going to show students a way to find out how big something is. Then, produce a ruler and measure the length of one of the books on your desk. After you have measured it, say, "Okay, my book is 12 inches long," and write that number on the whiteboard. Next, give a student the ruler and ask that student to measure another book of a different size and write that measurement on the whiteboard. Then ask the class, "Which book is bigger? Why?" As you ask that question, write it on the whiteboard. When students answer, write their responses under the question. Ask, "What can we say about things that are different sizes?" Also write that question on the whiteboard and solicit student responses. Figure 10.2 shows your questions and some sample student responses.

After you have solicited and written some student responses, stop and read them aloud to the class. Have individual students help you copy the students' responses onto sheets of construction paper. Have other students then take turns to illustrate the sheets with the students' responses. As a final step, attach the sheets of paper together and announce that now students have a book that they have written and illustrated about measuring things that are of different sizes. Place the book your class has made on a table for students to read.

Language Experience is very helpful not only for beginning writers, as in the previous example, but also for ELL students. As these students learn to connect their experiences to the written English word, they also get needed writing practice. Struggling writers also benefit from Language Experience; these students can use such activities to make vital connections between the way we express language verbally and the way we do so in written form.

Figure 10.2: Sample Student Responses

Which book is bigger?

"Your book is bigger, because it's longer."

"Your book, because it measured more."

"I think your book. It has a bigger number."

What can we say about things that are different sizes?

"Different sizes have different numbers."

"Bigger things have bigger numbers, and smaller things have smaller ones."

"You use a ruler to find out which one's bigger."

Conclusion

As we have seen, writing is an integral aspect of literacy. Classroom atmospheres that encourage and support writing also encourage students to write more often. This in turn leads to more skilled and sophisticated writing. So, it's to your advantage, and to that of your students, to plan many opportunities for students to express themselves in writing.

Writing can take many forms, both formal and informal. Informal, ungraded writing allows students to practice without the intimidation that sometimes results from knowing that one's work will be evaluated. More formal writing teaches students the skills they need to communicate in a variety of ways and to a variety of audiences. So it is helpful to your students to vary the kinds of writing they do.

In order for your students to develop as writers, it's vital that they have enough time to do so. This means setting aside time on a regular basis for students to write. It also means allowing students enough time to express their thoughts in writing. This is especially true when students are engaged in more long-term, formal work.

Chapter 10 Reflection

1. What sorts of writing do practitioners in your content area do? If
   you teach more than one subject, are there kinds of writing
   common to those subjects? How does this compare with the kinds
   of writing your students do in your class?

   _____

   _____

   _____

   _____

2. What sort of writing do you do yourself? How do you share your
   own writing with your students? (Remember, you're a role model!)

   _____

   _____

   _____

   _____

3. Review the section of this chapter that discusses the writing
   process. Which aspect of this process seems most challenging for
   your students? Which is the easiest? Why do you think this is the
   case?

   _____

   _____

   _____

   _____

Chapter
Eleven

Putting It All Together: Ways to Combine Strategies

Throughout this book, we have been discussing ways in which you can help your students derive meaning from their reading before they read, while they are reading, and after they have finished reading. Each of the strategies you have read about can be used to empower your students to engage in reading material at deeper levels. In this final chapter, we will discuss some strategies and approaches that you can use to combine various pre-reading, during-reading, and post-reading strategies to provide your students with a rich and meaningful reading experience.

Why Combine Strategies?

Before we discuss specific ways to combine reading comprehension strategies, it's important to consider the benefits that such a combination can offer your students. One advantage of combining strategies is that this approach helps students comprehend more successfully than using one strategy alone (Nolan, 1991). Combining strategies also allows you to develop a more comprehensive approach to integrating literacy into your content area. In this way, students' understanding of what they read is deepened by connecting it to prior knowledge before reading, active engagement with the material during reading, and extension of learning after reading.

Combining strategies need not be piecemeal; in fact, it's more productive to integrate strategies into a smooth and cohesive holistic approach to content area literacy. For this reason, the strategies described in this chapter integrate pre-, during-, and post-reading activities, rather than discussing these activities separately.

Integrated Strategies for Increased Comprehension

Let us examine some specific ways in which you can integrate strategies to help your students move toward a deeper and more independent comprehension of what they read.

Reciprocal Teaching

Reciprocal Teaching is perhaps the best-known of the integrated reading strategies. This approach to reading comprehension was developed by Palincsar and Brown (1986), who found that Reciprocal Teaching helped students to better comprehend what they read and to better monitor their comprehension. Reciprocal Teaching begins with the teacher coaching students on four skills for comprehension monitoring: clarifying, predicting, summarizing, and questioning. Once students have learned these skills, they take turns (usually in small groups) being the "teacher," as other students in those groups use these skills to derive meaning from their reading. The goal here is for students to learn to monitor their own understanding of what they read.

Reciprocal Teaching can be implemented in different ways. What follows is an example of one way in which you might integrate this approach into your own content area. Suppose your third-grade students are studying the forms that matter can take (solid, liquid, gas). They are about to read a section in their science texts that describes the process by which water can change its form. Begin class by reminding students that they have been learning about matter and telling them that they are going to read about one kind of matter—water. Then list four words on the whiteboard—*Clarify, Predict, Summarize, Question*—and ask student volunteers to tell you what these words mean. After individual students have defined the words, explain that these four skills are going to help them better understand what they read. Then, have your students open their texts to the section they are going to read, while you do the same with your text. After glancing at the headings and subheadings in the text, point to the word *Predict* on the whiteboard and say, "I'm going to make a prediction: this section is going to tell me what happens to water when it's heated. Does anyone else have a prediction?" After a few students offer you a prediction, tell the students that you are all going to read the passage to find out if your predictions are correct. You and the class then begin taking turns reading the passage aloud. After the first few sentences, stop, point to the word *Question* on the whiteboard, and ask, "Does anyone have a question?" When a student asks a question, ask if anyone knows the answer. After the answer has been found, continue reading the passage. After the next few sentences, stop the class, point to the word *Clarify* on the whiteboard and ask if anyone needs anything to be clarified. If clarification is needed, ask if anyone can help clarify. Once the clarification has been provided, return to the passage and continue sharing the reading. After you are finished with the passage, stop, point to the word *Summarize* on the whiteboard and say, "Who can tell me in their own words what this passage was about?" When a few student volunteers provide summaries say, "Okay, were our predictions right?" End this activity with a brief review of the skills you all used in understanding the passage.

At the next class session, remind the students of the skills they used to read about changes in matter and tell them that they are going to use the same skills again, only this time in small groups. Place your students in small groups and hand each group a copy of the list of the four skills they will use. Indicate who will be the first "teacher" in each group and explain that the teacher's job is to make sure that everyone gets a chance to read and to use those four skills. Then have students begin to read the next passage in their science texts. As students read within their groups, walk around the room to ensure that students are using the four skills you have taught them and that each group's teacher is facilitating the group's activities. End this activity with a brief whole-class summary of the passage.

Collaborative Strategic Reading (CSR)

Reciprocal Teaching is only one way to approach a comprehensive integration of reading strategies. Another, which also helps students learn to monitor their own comprehension, is Collaborative Strategic Reading (CSR) (Klingner & Vaughn, 1998). Students use this strategy to preview a text before they read it to distinguish between what they do and do not understand as they read and to review after they have read. The teacher first coaches students on how to use CSR; later, students use this strategy in small groups. CSR can be broken down into the following components:

- **Preview**

  In this stage, students glance over the text they are about to read and then generate ideas about what they already know about the topic. They also make predictions about what they are going to learn about the topic as they read.

- **Click and Chunk**

  This phase of CSR takes place while students are reading. "Click" refers to the student's awareness that he/she understands the reading and that everything makes sense. When students encounter a word or phrase that confuses them, this is called a "Chunk." Here, students are taught to go back and reread, search for context clues, and otherwise repair the misunderstanding.

- **Get the Gist**

  This strategy also takes place during reading. Here, students are taught to look for the most important item, person, place, or idea being discussed. They are also taught to identify the most important things that are mentioned about the main topic.

- **Wrap-Up**

  After students are finished reading, they generate questions and answers that show they have understood what they read. Some teachers have students pretend they are the teacher and write questions about the passage that they would ask their students.

After students have learned to use CSR as a whole class, they are ready to use this strategy in small groups. Within each group, students take turns assuming different roles designed to ensure that everyone has a chance to participate, that the group's findings are recorded, and that the group completes the reading and associated tasks on time.

CSR can be adapted for a variety of content areas. Let us now look at a way you might adapt CSR in a mathematics class. Suppose your students are learning how to solve long division problems through the algorithmic process. You have demonstrated this process to your class and now your students have the background information they need to read the section of the text that describes solving long division problems. Place your students in small groups and ask each group to use CSR to read the relevant section in their texts. Let us take a look at how one small group might accomplish this task:

Group Leader: Okay, we're supposed to read this section. So, what do we already know about long division? (*Preview*)

Student A: Well, isn't that what we just did on the whiteboard?

Student B: Yeah, it is. So we already know the steps, or at least we saw them.

Group Leader: Yes, we did. So I think this section is just going to talk about how to do those steps and give us examples.

Student C: So is that our prediction?

Students A and B: Yeah.

Group Leader: Okay, so who wants to start reading?

Student A: I guess I will. (Student begins to read aloud.)

Student B: Wait a minute; I don't get it (*Chunk*). What's that word?

Group Leader: Let's go back and look . . . oh, here it is. Long division problems are solved following a certain number of steps (the algorithmic process).

Student B: Okay, I remember. (Student continues to read.)

Group Leader: (After a short time) So what's the main point here? (*Get the Gist*)

Student C: I think it's the steps you use to solve long division problems. That's what the whole passage talks about.

Student A: I think so, too.

Group Leader: Okay, so that's our Gist, I guess. (After students have finished reading)

Group Leader: What questions are we going to ask? (*Wrap-Up*)

Student B: How about, "What are the steps to solve long division problems?"

Student A: Okay, we can use that. Couldn't we also say, "Solve these problems," and make them long division problems?

Group Leader: I guess so, but I like asking what the steps are better, because if you don't know the steps, you can't solve the problems.

Student C: Yeah, I agree. (The small group session ends as the group writes its question and prepares to share it with the class.)

Question/Answer Relationships (QAR)

As you read in Chapter 9, QAR provides students with a structure for developing their ability to use their texts to ask and answer questions. We mention QAR again here chiefly because this strategy also serves as a self-monitoring strategy that students can use before they read, while they are reading, and after they have finished reading. When students focus on how and where to find the answers to questions (see Figure 9.2 on page 125), they are also monitoring their own comprehension.

Like other comprehensive strategies, the goal of QAR is to empower students to independently prepare to read, actively engage the text while they are reading, and review what they have learned after they read. While other strategies make use of such skills as summarizing, QAR emphasizes questioning. Students may not have experience at generating their own questions, especially questions that go beyond the Knowledge level (see Figure 9.1 on page 118). So as you prepare to integrate QAR, you will want to first coach your students to use the strategy and then give them opportunities to use it under your guidance and, later, on their own.

Directed Reading and Thinking Activity (DRTA)

Like the other comprehensive strategies described here, DRTA (Stauffer, 1975) is designed to engage students actively before they read, while they read, and after they have finished reading. DRTA combines prediction (see Chapter 4) and questioning (see Chapter 9) skills to help students establish and focus on a purpose for reading. To implement DRTA, the teacher begins by having the students glance at the text they will be reading and use illustrations, titles, subheadings, and graphics to make a prediction about what the topic of the text will be. Here, the teacher also has students explain how they arrived at their prediction. Next, the students begin to read the text; when they get to a logical stopping point, the teacher has the students think about their predictions and either maintain or revise them. If a student chooses to revise his/her prediction, the teacher has the student explain his/her revision. After this review of predictions, the class continues reading, stopping again at the next logical breaking point for another review of predictions. This process continues until the passage is complete.

As a concrete example of DRTA, consider this scenario. Your fourth-grade students are learning about igneous, sedimentary, and metamorphic rocks and the processes that form them. Remind the class that they have been reading about rocks and ask them to turn to the section in their texts that describes the processes by which different kinds of rocks are formed. Then, ask the students to look at the title of the section and the pictures they see, and say, "Okay, we've looked at the titles and pictures; who can use them to predict what this section is going to be about?" A student tells you, "Well, those are pictures of rocks, so I think it's going to be about different kinds of rocks." Another says, "Yeah, and each section has a different name, so I guess those are going to be the names of the rocks they talk about." You say, "Those are good predictions. Let's see if you're right." You and the class then begin to read the passage, taking turns as you read. At the end of the first section, stop and say, "Okay, let's think about those predictions we made. Were they right?" When students verify their predictions, say, "How do you know?", and have students use what they have read to support their answers. Then move on to the next section in the passage and repeat the prediction-verification process at the end of that section. When the reading for the day is finished, ask the students to use their predictions to generate some summary sentences to remind them of what the passage was about. The activity ends as you have the students write those sentences in their journals.

Conclusion

As we have seen throughout this book, integrating a wide variety of strategies for active reading is beneficial to you and to your students. Using these strategies helps you to understand your students' thought processes and mental representations of what they are reading. It also allows you to coach and model effective comprehension strategies. Your students benefit from these strategies, too. Comprehension strategies empower your students to access their prior knowledge, make connections to it while they are reading, and monitor their comprehension while they read and after they read.

These strategies are useful enough by themselves; they are even more beneficial when used in combination. Combining strategies helps students see that reading is a comprehensive process that begins before one actually reads and continues even after one is finished reading. Comprehensive strategies such as the ones described in this chapter also help students move from teacher-directed reading activities to independent reading and comprehension monitoring. Finally, comprehensive reading strategies are flexible enough to be useful for narrative and expository text in a wide variety of content areas. So it is to everyone's advantage for your students to have opportunities to use strategies that combine the best of pre-reading, during-reading, and post-reading activities.

Chapter 11 Reflection

1. How do you use predictions to understand what you are about to read? How do you use self-questioning?

_____

_____

_____

_____

2. What are some ways in which you gradually move your students from teacher-directed to independent reading? Do you use whole-class sessions followed by small-group sessions? Individual coaching? Pair work?

_____

_____

_____

_____

3. Which combination of strategies do you find most useful in helping your students move toward improved comprehension? Why are these successful?

_____

_____

_____

_____

Glossary

active reading—engaging a text in a purposeful way

advance organizer—a mental structure used to associate new material in meaningful ways

Bloom's Taxonomy—a hierarchy of question types, ranging from knowledge-level to evaluation-level questions

Collaborative Strategic Reading (CSR)—a comprehensive reading strategy that involves previewing a text, monitoring comprehension while one reads, and reviewing after one has read

cooperative learning—a teaching and learning approach in which students work together in pairs or small groups and learn from one another

discussion—a form of verbal collaboration in which ideas are shared and refined

expository text—reading material that serves the purpose of providing information (e.g., a textbook)

graphic organizer—a visual way to depict and categorize information

Language Experience—a writing strategy in which students' own words are used as the basis for creating material that students will later read and use for review

narrative text—reading material that serves the purpose of telling a story (e.g., a novel)

prior knowledge—information that the reader already has about a topic before he/she reads

Question/Answer Relationships (QAR)—a strategy designed to help students learn where to find the answers to different types of questions (text explicit, text implicit, and script implicit)

questioning—a strategy used to set a purpose for reading through searching for answers within a text

Reciprocal Teaching—a comprehensive reading strategy designed to help the reader use questions, summaries, predictions, and clarifications to better understand a text

scaffold—a temporary support provided to a reader as he/she develops independent reading skills

schema—a mental representation of a concept

semantic mapping—using a graphic organizer to depict the relationships among a set of ideas or concepts

situated learning—learning that takes place within a particular context

summarizing—a strategy used to help the reader distill the most important facts or ideas from a passage

think-aloud—a strategy designed to model expert reading practice by having the expert verbalize his/her thought processesproblem-based learning activity

References

Allen, J. (1999). *Words, words, words: Teaching vocabulary in grades 4–12.* Portland, ME: Stenhouse.

Alvermann, D., & Hayes, D. (1989). Classroom discussion of content area reading assignments: An intervention study. *Reading Research Quarterly, 24(3),* 305–335.

Anderson, R., & Pearson, P. D. (1984). A schema-theoretic view of basic processes in reading comprehension. In P. D. Pearson (Ed.), *Handbook of reading research* (pp. 255–291). New York: Longman.

Applefield, J., Huber, R., & Moallem, M. (2001). Constructivism in theory and practice: Toward a better understanding. *The High School Journal, 84(2),* 35–53.

Ausubel, D. (1968). *Educational psychology: A cognitive view.* New York: Holt, Rinehart, and Winston.

Baumann, J. (1984). The effectiveness of a direct instruction paradigm for teaching main idea comprehension. *Reading Research Quarterly, 20,* 93–108.

Beck, I., & McKeown, M. (1981). Developing questions that promote comprehension: The story map. *Language Arts, 58(8),* 913–918.

Beck, I., McKeown, M., Hamilton, R., & Kucan, L. (1997). *Questioning the author: An approach for enhancing student engagement with text.* Newark, DE: International Reading Association.

Beck, I., McKeown, M., & Kucan, L. (2002). *Bringing words to life: Robust vocabulary instruction.* New York: Guilford.

Blachowicz, C., Fisher, P., & Watts-Taffe, S. (2005). *Integrated vocabulary instruction: Meeting the needs of diverse learners in grades K–5.* Naperville, IL: Learning Point Associates.

Bloom, B. (1984). *Taxonomy of educational objectives.* Boston: Allyn & Bacon.

Bromley, K., & Mannix, D. (1993). Beyond the classroom: Publishing student work in magazines. In T. Rasinski, N. Padak, B. Church, G. Fawcett, J. Hendershot, J. Henry, B. Moss, J. Peck, E. Pryor, & K. Roskos (Eds.), *Developing reading-writing connections: Strategies from "The Reading Teacher"* (pp. 154–161). Newark, DE: International Reading Association.

Brown, A., Campione, J., & Day, J. (1981). Learning to learn: On training students to learn from text. *Educational Researcher, 10(2),* 14–21.

Brown, J. S., Collins, A., & Duguid, P. (1989). Situated cognition and the culture of learning. *Educational Researcher, 18(1),* 32–42.

Carr, E., & Ogle, D. (1987). K-W-L plus: A strategy for comprehension and summarization. *Journal of Reading, 30(7),* 626–631.

Cummins, J. (1994). Primary language instruction and the education of minority language students. In C. F. Leyba (Ed.), *Schooling and language minority students: A theoretical framework* (pp. 3–46). Los Angeles: Evaluation Dissemination and Assessment Center, School of Education, California State University.

Cunningham, J. W. (1982). Generating interactions between schemata and text. In J. Niles & L. Harris (Eds.), *New inquiries in reading research and instruction* (pp. 42–47). Newark, DE: International Reading Association.

Cunningham, P. (1999). *Classrooms that work* (2nd ed.). New York: Addison Wesley.

De Temple, J., & Tabors, P. (1996, August). *Children's story retelling as a predictor of early reading achievement.* Paper presented at the 14th biennial meeting of the International Society for the Study of Behavioral Development. Quebec City, Quebec, Canada.

Duffelmeyer, F. (1994). Effective anticipation guide statements for learning from expository prose. *Journal of Reading, 37,* 452–455.

Duke, N. K. (2004). The case for informational text. *Educational Leadership 61(6),* 41–44.

Duke, N. K., & Bennett-Armistead, V. S. (2003). *Reading and writing informational text in the primary grades: Research-based practices.* New York: Scholastic.

Edler, K. (1988). *The effect of using predictions on a reader's comprehension.* Unpublished master's thesis, University of Toledo, Ohio.

Frayer, D. A., Frederick, W. C., & Klausmeier, H. G. (1969). *A schema for testing the level of concept mastery* (Tech. Rep. No. 16). Madison: University of Wisconsin, Wisconsin Center for Education Research.

Gardner, H. (1999). *Intelligence reframed: Multiple intelligences for the 21st century.* New York: Basic Books.

Gau, E., Hermanson, J., Logar, M., & Smerek, C. (2003). *Improving student attitudes and writing abilities through increased writing times and opportunities.* Unpublished master's research project, St. Xavier University, Chicago, Illinois.

Harvey, S., & Goudvis, A. (2005). *The comprehension toolkit: Language and lessons for active literacy.* Portsmouth, NH: Heinemann.

Hibbing, A., & Rank-Erickson, J. (2003). A picture is worth a thousand words: Using visual images to improve comprehension for middle school struggling readers. *The Reading Teacher, 56(8),* 758–770.

Hillocks, G. (2005). The focus on form vs. content in the teaching of writing. *Research in the Teaching of English, 40(2),* 238–249.

Hornea, J. (1982). Wait-time as an instructional variable: An influence on teacher and student. *The Clearing House, 56(4),* 167–170.

Hoyt, L. (2002). *Making it real: Strategies for success with informational texts.* Portsmouth, NH: Heinemann.

Hutchins, P. (1989). *The doorbell rang.* New York: HarperTrophy.

Kameenui, E. (1993). Diverse learners and the tyranny of time: Don't fix blame; fix the leaky roof. *The Reading Teacher 46(5),* 376–383.

Kim, A. (2002). Effects of computer-assisted collaborative strategic reading on reading comprehension for high school students with learning disabilities. (Doctoral dissertation, The University of Texas at Austin, 2002). *Dissertation Abstracts International, 64*, 4009.

King, A. (1990). Enhancing peer interaction and learning in the classroom through reciprocal questioning. *American Educational Research Journal, 27(4)*, 664–687.

Klingner, J., & Vaughn, S. (1998). Using collaborative strategic reading. *Teaching Exceptional Children, 30(6)*, 32–38.

Krashen, S. (1994). Bilingual education and second language acquisition theory. In C. Leyba (Ed.), *Schooling and language minority students: A theoretical framework* (pp. 47–75). Los Angeles: Evaluation Dissemination and Assessment Center, School of Education, California State University.

Lave, J. (1997). The culture of acquisition and the practice of understanding. In D. Kirschner & J. Whitson (Eds.), *Situated cognition: Social, semiotic, and psychological perspectives* (pp. 17–35). Mahwah, NJ: Lawrence Erlbaum.

Lester, J., Head, M., Elliott, C., Simoneaux, D., & Trowbridge, J. (2001). *Literacy and learning: Reading in the content areas (Handbook III)*. Baton Rouge, LA: Louisiana Public Broadcasting.

Malone, L., & Mastropieri, M. (1991). Reading comprehension instruction: Summarization and self-monitoring training for students with learning disabilities. *Exceptional Children, 58(3)*, 270–280.

Manz, S. (2002). A strategy for previewing textbooks: Teaching readers to become THIEVES. *The Reading Teacher, 55(5)*, 434–435.

Manzo, A. (1969). The ReQuest procedure. *Journal of Reading, 13(2)*, 123–126.

Marzano, R., Pickering, D., & Pollock, J. (2001). *Classroom instruction that works: Research-based strategies for increasing student achievement.* Alexandria, VA: McCrel.

McKeatchie, W. (1999). *Teaching tips* (10th Ed.). Boston: Houghton Mifflin.

McKenna, M. (2002). *Help for struggling readers: Strategies for grades K–8.* New York: Guilford Press.

Mealy, D., & Nist, S. (1989). Postsecondary teacher directed comprehension strategies. *Journal of Reading, 32(6),* 484–493.

Middendorf, J., & Kalish, A. (1996, January). The "change-up" in lectures. *The National Teaching and Learning Forum, 5(2).* Retrieved on March 26, 2006, from http://www.ntlf.com/html/pi/9601/article1.htm

Miner, A., & Reder, L. (1996). A new look at feeling and knowing: Its metacognitive role in regulating question answering. In J. Metcalf & A. Shinamura (Eds.), *Metacognition: Knowing about knowing* (pp. 47–70). Cambridge, MA: MIT Press.

Moore, D. W., & Moore, S. A. (1992). Possible sentences: An update. In E. K. Dishner, T. W. Bean, J. E. Readence, & D. W. Moore (Eds.), *Reading in the content areas: Improving classroom instruction* (3rd ed., pp. 196–202). Dubuque, IA: Kendall/Hunt.

Munsch, R. (1980). *The paper bag princess.* Toronto, Canada: Annick Press.

Nagy, W. E., & Scott, J. A. (2000). Vocabulary processes. In M. L. Kamil, P. B. Mosenthal, P. D. Pearson, & R. Barr (Eds.), *Handbook of reading research* (Vol. 3, pp. 269–284). Mahwah, NJ: Lawrence Erlbaum.

National Reading Panel (2000). *Teaching children to read: An evidence-based assessment of the scientific research literature on reading and its implications for reading instruction.* Washington, DC: National Institute of Child Health and Human Development.

Nolan, T. (1991). Self-questioning and prediction: Combining metacognitive strategies. *Journal of Reading, 35(2),*132–138.

Ogle, D. (1986). The KWL: A teaching model that develops active reading of expository text. *The Reading Teacher, 39(6),* 564–570.

Oster, L. (2001). Using the think-aloud for reading instruction. *The Reading Teacher, 55(1),* 64–69.

Palincsar, A., & Brown, A. (1986). Interactive teaching to promote independent learning from text. *The Reading Teacher, 39(8)*, 771–777.

Paris, S., Wasik, B., & Turner, J. (1991). The development of strategic readers. In R. Barr, M. L. Kamil, P. Mosenthal, & P. D. Pearson (Eds.), *Handbook of reading research*, (Vol. 2, pp. 609–640). Mahwah, NJ: Lawrence Erlbaum.

Piaget, J. (1950). *The psychology of intelligence.* London: Routledge & Kegan Paul.

Pressley, M. (2002). Metacognition and self-regulated comprehension. In A. Farstrup & J. Samuels (Eds.), *What research has to say about reading instruction* (3rd ed., pp. 291–309). Newark, DE: International Reading Association.

Preul, K., & Dewitz, P. (1986, December). *The effectiveness of a self-monitoring strategy for teaching reading comprehension.* Paper presented at the annual meeting of the National Reading Conference, Austin, Texas.

Richards, J., & Anderson N. (2003). How do you know? A strategy to help emergent readers make inferences. *The Reading Teacher, 57(3)*, 290–293.

Richgels, D., McGee, L., & Slaton, E. (1989). Teaching expository text structure in reading and writing. In K. D. Muth (Ed.), *Children's comprehension of text* (pp. 167–184). Newark, DE: International Reading Association.

Rogers, S., Ludington, J., & Graham, S. (1999). *Motivation and learning: A teacher's guide to building excitement for learning and igniting the drive for quality.* Evergreen, CO: Peak Learning Systems.

Rupley, W., Logan, J., & Nichols, W. (1999). Vocabulary instruction in a balanced reading program. *The Reading Teacher, 52(4)*, 336–347.

Ryder, R., & Graves, M. (2003). *Reading and learning in content areas* (3rd ed.). New York: John Wiley & Sons.

Sasaki, M. (2000). Effects of cultural schemata on students' test-taking processes for cloze tests: A multiple data source approach. *Language Testing, 17(1)*, 85–114.

Schoenfield, A. (1985). *Mathematical problem solving.* New York: Academic Press.

Scott, Foresman & Company (2003). *Science: Grade 4.* Upper Saddle River, NJ: Pearson Scott Foresman.

Skinner, E., & Belmont, M. (1993). Motivation in the classroom: Reciprocal effects of teacher behavior and student engagement across the school year. *Journal of Educational Psychology, 85(4)*, 571–581.

Sorrell, A. (1996, October). *A triarchic approach to reading comprehension strategy instruction.* Paper presented at the annual conference of the Learning Disabilities Association of Texas, Austin.

Stanovich, K. (1986). Matthew effects in reading: Some consequences of individual differences in the acquisition of literacy. *Reading Research Quarterly, 21(4)*, 360–407.

Stauffer, R. (1975). *Directing the direct reading-thinking process.* New York: Harper & Row.

Strickland, R. (1969). *The language arts in the elementary school.* Lexington, MA: D.C. Heath and Company.

Texas Education Agency (2002). *Comprehension instruction.* Austin: Texas Education Agency.

U.S. Census Bureau (2005). *Computer and internet use in the United States: 2003.* Washington, DC: U.S. Census Bureau.

Vacca, R., & Linek, W. (1992). Writing to learn. In J. Irwin & M. Doyle (Eds.), *Reading/writing connections: Learning from research* (pp. 145–159). Newark, DE: International Reading Association.

Wilson, C. (1999, June). *Using pictures in EFL and ESL classrooms.* Paper presented at the Current Trends in English Language Testing Conference, Abu Dhabi, United Arab Emirates.

Wood, K., & Endres, C. (2004). Motivating student interest with the imagine, elaborate, predict, and confirm (IEPC) strategy. *The Reading Teacher, 58(4)*, 346–357.

Notes